FUNNY HOW
LIFE
HOW
WORKS

MICHAEL JR.

BREAKFAST
FOR SEVEN

TABLE OF CONTENTS

FOREWORD

I had just settled into my chair on the front row and was looking forward to hearing a comedian I'd heard good things about but had never seen perform. On this night in 2011, Michael Jr. was bringing his act to a huge church auditorium, rather than to some intimate little comedy club.

Soon, to my surprise, a staff member approached me with a question. "Michael Jr. noticed you taking your seat from backstage and wondered if you would be open to joining him on stage so he could interview you." As I would later learn, Michael had read several of my books and was familiar with quite a few of my seminars and talks. Up until that moment, I hadn't known that I could count among my leadership students a comic who had appeared on *The Tonight Show*, among other high-profile venues.

I was confused and reticent. I wasn't at all sure what I was getting myself into, but I agreed. In short order, two chairs appeared on the stage and I was fitted with a clip-on microphone. Soon I found myself sitting across from a brilliant improvisational comic fielding loaded questions I was hearing for the very first time. And doing so in front of 4,000 people!

I knew I was in trouble as soon as I heard the very first question:

"Now, John, you wrote a book called, *The 360 Degree Leader*?"

"Yes, that's correct," I answered. I began to relax just a little. *Okay, he's going to ask me about my books. That's good! I can do this!*

"So," Michael continued. "if someone becomes a 360-degree leader, doesn't that mean they'll just end up right back where they started?"

The audience roared, and I burst out laughing, too. Over the next few minutes I had the best seat in the house for observing a truly gifted communicator do his thing, as my book titles and leadership philosophies served as the springboard for a series of cleverly improvised jokes. But it was all done with graciousness and warmth. He made it fun for me to be his straight man. That's one of the things that distinguishes Michael's comedy from that of a lot of other successful comics. His humor possesses no mean streak. And neither does he. What comes through is that he genuinely cares about people. In the years since, it's been my pleasure to count Michael Jr. as a friend and colleague.

Michael and I might have more in common than you might first assume. As you may be aware, I'm known primarily as a writer and speaker on the subject of leadership. Michael, on the other hand, makes people laugh. And he's very good at it.

Now there might seem to be a wide difference between those two callings, but both require standing up in front large groups of complete strangers and finding a way to quickly connect to their hearts. As it turns out, humor is one of the most powerfully connective things in the world. Few things can cause us to lower the defensive shields we all tend to erect around our hearts as can laughter.

Yes, humor is powerful. But it is also extraordinarily tricky. The line between amusing someone and offending them is so thin, it's sometimes impossible for the unskilled eye to see. To be honest, I'm in awe of successful comedians. Success in comedy is one of the most difficult things in the world to pull off. It requires high levels of intelligence, empathy, and insight into the human soul to craft great jokes and then, in real time, read an audience to know which joke to tell next and which one to skip. Do it well, however, and you'll have an open door to influence. And there is no leadership without influence.

In my book *The 21 Irrefutable Laws of Leadership*, the tenth of these was "The Law of Connection," and it begins by explaining that "Leaders touch a heart before they ask for a hand." Michael Jr. is a remarkable leader because he has mastered the art of touching hearts with humor.

That's why I'm so happy he's chosen to share some of his hard-earned wisdom and insight in the pages of this book. Like the very best teachers, Michael embeds his wisdom into stories. We quickly forget information.

Inspiration often fades. But *stories* stay with us forever. Michael's stories, accumulated throughout his own unusual journey, reveal important truths you and I can absorb and apply to make our lives better, and to improve the lives of everyone around us. And, of course, you'll find yourself laughing out loud as you read.

—John Maxwell

INTRODUCTION

I'm so glad that you've decided to read this book. I know from years of experience that when people laugh, their hearts are open and that's the perfect time to make a deposit that can help them in some way. My desire for you in reading this book is that through my account of my life stories and situations that some laughter and even light could be shed into your life, and maybe even a situation that you and a loved one are in. If a deposit can be made that can help you through, then we both win. Whatever is deposited in your heart will be revealed in your walk.

Enjoy this video where I explain the premise behind *Funny How Life Works* and the best way to read it. I hope that by the connections made in my stories, you will be able to make similar connections in your own lives. Hold your camera phone up to this QR code to watch . . . unless you've got a flip phone—which is a different conversation. In which case you can just go to *FunnyHowLifeWorks.com/intro*.

CHAPTER 1

60 CENTS AND AN ORANGE

It's funny how life works as a great teacher, not overly eager to give us instructions, but patient enough to allow the circumstances to reveal the needed lesson. The things you learn, or go through, in one area of life can prepare you for something else that, at first glance, is completely unrelated. These lessons start in childhood. I'll never forget what I learned as a nine-year-old boy growing up in Grand Rapids, Michigan.

When I was a kid, the type of bike you rode was pretty important. It wasn't so much how you keep up with your friends from a status symbol perspective, it was literally how you kept up with your friends. See, all the boys in my neighborhood had dirt bikes and we didn't ride anywhere . . . we raced everywhere. This is the primary way that we competed to find out who was best and who was less. We didn't have iPads, Xboxes, and PlayStations to feed our need to compete, so this was truly how we rode.

There were about seven of us who rolled together most of the time; and even though we are grown men now, I'm pretty sure that none of us have forgotten when my cousin, one of the seven, showed up with a brand spanking new BMX Predator. None of us had even seen one in real life before; we had only heard rumors of its existence. At 9 years old I just thought it was a myth, like the Loch Ness Monster, Bigfoot, or a poor white person. You have to understand, the Predator was the Bentley of dirt bikes: chrome frame, aluminum rims, AME grips with rat trap pedals, and Snakebelly tires. Even more impressive than the way it looked was the way it rode. My cousin could give just half a pedal and that Predator seemed to glide for like half a block.

My bike was definitely not in the Predator class, or school, or even the same school district. And if at any point my bike was in the same school as my cousin's, it would have been the result of an experiment in shop class. My ingenuity was the only thing keeping this hoopty together. ("Hoopty" is a word we used in my neighborhood that meant at one time the thing may have been nice but could never be that way again.) I used spare parts, duct tape, creativity, and prayer to build what my friends referred to as "Schwuffy-else." It was made from a burgundy Schwinn, a silver Huffy, and whatever else I could find.

Unlike my cousin's gliding Predator, my Schwuffy-else churned loudly and slowly down the streets. You know how old people make noises when they stand up? Well imagine what old people would sound like if they were made out of metal and were trying to make their way down the street with a nine-year-old on their back. This is about what my bike sounded like. I pedaled twice as hard to go half as fast as my friends. It got to the point where I could recognize my friends better by the back of their heads than by their faces.

I needed a new bike, one that didn't creak and groan, and I decided the Predator was the answer to all my problems.

I'll never forget going to my dad and asking him for a new bicycle. I must have had 100 pounds of enthusiasm and 3 tons of hesitation as I poked my chest out and slowly lifted my head until my eyes were looking directly into his lower chin, well upper neck area really. Listen okay, I was thinking eye contact in my head, but the upper neck was as far as I could get and may have been a new record, so stop judging. "Dad, will you buy me a new bike . . . a Predator?"

He stared at me for 18 minutes straight, really maybe 2 seconds, and I heard the voiceover of the kid from the TV show *Wonder Years* say, "Boy was this a mistake." He looked down at me and asked gruffly, "How much does it cost?"

"It's just like two hundred dollars," I gulped.

Dad paused for another 18 minutes and I was prepared for a resounding "no" and braced for the realization that it would probably be me and Schwuffy-else until I got my learners permit.

My dad said, "I'll tell you what . . ." We need to pause right here for at least a moment. You don't understand how big a deal his phrase was. It was equal to Flavor Flav saying to Halle Berry, "I know we just met, and I don't speak clear English, and most times I wear a kitchen clock as jewelry, but would you like to marry me?" And she would reply, "Let me think about it." Yeah, that's what that was like. My dad actually said, "If you raise half the money, I'll chip in the other half."

Boom! Yes! I could do that. How hard could it be? I was so excited, and I got to work right away doing what all midwestern kids do to earn money in the winter— shovel snow.

Luckily for me, we got six inches of fluffy white snow the night before, so the job opportunities were endless. I knew that my first client could be Mrs. Elmer, the elderly lady next door. I knew she probably couldn't shovel her own snow; she was probably way too old. When she would tell me a Bible story it sometimes would include the phrase, "And then I turned to Jesus and said . . ." Anyways, she agreed; sweet Mrs. Elmer agreed to be my first customer. I worked tirelessly shoveling a mountain of snow from her porch, sidewalk, and driveway. The work was grueling, but I just kept thinking about how much money I was going to make. That Predator was as good as mine.

When I finished shoveling, her porch, sidewalk, and driveway were in perfect condition. I was so proud of the job I had done. Now it was time to get paid. I knocked proudly on the front door to report that the job was completed.

There is no easy way to say what happened next . . .

After a quick inspection and a pat on the back, Mrs. Elmer reached into her purse and pulled out 60 cents and an orange. She smiled, as if to say, "Don't spend it all in one place," handed me the fruit and spare change, and sent me on my way.

Sixty cents and an orange! What!? I was now sweating more than I was from shoveling the snow. I was completely furious, but I still had almost enough wits to not be mean or in any way disrespectful. But the whole time I'm thinking, *How could she think so little of my work?* I went home and complained to my dad: "It's not fair," I griped. "I'm never going to earn $100 if I keep getting paid in produce!"

I don't know what I expected. Maybe there was a part of me that thought my dad would go over to her house and demand a raise in pay. Or maybe I just wanted him to join me in my frustration. He didn't do either of those things. Instead, he said, "Son, you learned a lesson today. Never do a job without negotiating a price first."

I was ready to quit right there. I was so disappointed and angry that I could have easily given up. My work wasn't appreciated, life seemed unfair, and instead of being closer to the Predator, I felt like the prey. Why keep trying?

Let me pause at this point in my story to ask you a question: *Have you ever found yourself in a similar situation?* You probably haven't been paid from the produce section recently, but have you ever found yourself disappointed? Ever felt underappreciated? Ever felt like life wasn't fair or that your goal was just out of reach?

If you have, you know that it's very tempting to give up, to stop trying all together.

> Despair and disappointment have a way of sapping our strength and ambushing our ambition. But allow me to suggest that maybe something deeper is happening through the struggle. Perhaps you're learning a lesson that is actually preparing you, developing you, and equipping you for something else down the road.

Maybe all the hard peddling was strengthening your legs for the hill you couldn't see coming. Your current problem could be teaching you something that propels you into something bigger and better.

My story doesn't end with me crying on the couch while trying to peel an orange. (If possible, you should play the *Rocky V* theme song in your head while you read the next two sentences.) I decided not to give up. Instead, I went back into the neighborhood on that cold, snowy Michigan day and shoveled my heart out. I went from house to house, negotiated fair prices, and pushed the snow back and slung rock salt until sundown. You should have seen me—I was like the brown Energizer Bunny of snow shovelers.

When I walked into my house, well after dark, I pulled the crinkled money from my pockets and counted my wages with hands raw from their labor. When I finished counting, I couldn't believe it. Surely this had to be a mistake. I counted again to make sure. Nope, there was no mistake. This was unbelievable. Laid out on the couch in front of me, right beside an orange I would never eat, was ninety-one dollars. To a nine-year-old kid, ninety-one dollars might as well have been 9 million dollars. I was rich!

I think my dad was as surprised as I was. And he was proud. So proud, in fact, that he said, "Michael, you're close enough to halfway. I'll pay the rest. Tomorrow morning, let's go get that bike you want."

But life had taught me another lesson that day: the importance of hard work and the value of a dollar. Before

I spent the entire day fighting Mother Nature, money was arbitrary, just words . . . just an idea. But now? Now that I had spent my sweat and bent my back working for it, money had a different importance. There was no way I was going to spend it all in one place at one time.

"Thanks, Dad, but I don't want the Predator anymore. I'm going to spend a few dollars to fix up Schwuffy-else and save the rest." And that's exactly what I did.

That was a big day for me, one that I still mention on stage from time to time. You see, a day that started with dreadful disappointment ended with new knowledge. Life had taught me a few lessons that day. Lessons I still hold on to today as a comedian. Comedy doesn't happen just because you're funny. It takes work, dedication, and commitment to make a career as a comedian. It may look like someone just takes the stage and starts rattling off jokes, but it takes a lot of discipline behind the scenes if a comedian is going to make it long term.

> I didn't know it at the time, but at 9 years old, I was learning lessons that would serve me later in life and not just as a comedian.

What about you? Is it possible that the grind you find yourself in now is actually teaching you something that you can use later in life? For example: If you've got a selfish, irritating boss, the easy way out is to tell them off and quit in dramatic fashion. But before you go all Yosemite Sam on them, ask yourself, *What is it I can learn from this situation that could serve me or others now, or in my future?*

Maybe you're in a position right now where your finances are tight, where your cashflow isn't flowing. The temptation is to feel sorry for yourself, blame the economy, and hit that credit card. But this can actually be a learning opportunity. This is a chance to build a budget and examine expenses. If you can handle your checkbook when times are tight, think about how successful you'll be when it's financially better in the future.

I don't know exactly what challenges you're facing, but I do know that everything you face—no matter how good or how bad—can be used for your good.

> If you'll have a mindset that is open to learn from your experiences, the obstacles of today can become the opportunities of tomorrow.

That difficult relationship, that job struggle, that disappointing outcome, that missed opportunity—it's not the end. It's something you can look back on and realize it prepared you for something better. Embrace it. Learn from it. It's your very own "60 Cents and an Orange" story.

CHAPTER 2

AN UNOPENED GIFT

I once heard it said that a "friend" is someone who will help you move. A "best friend" is someone who will help you move a body.

I had a friend like that back in the day, when I was a kid growing up in Michigan. His name was Dwayne, and you could say we were like two pees in a pod, but we didn't have a pod to pee in, so let's just say we were homies. For my ebonically challenged readers, that's a friend who has your back no matter what. That's who Dwayne was for me and who I was for him, all through our grade school and teenage years.

> We did everything together; and like most teenage dudes who think they are invincible, we competed against each other constantly to confirm who was the best, at whatever.

And I can tell you I was better than him at every single challenge, and the reason I can tell you this as fact is because I'm the one writing this book. But for the sake of this chapter, and the fact that most likely he will hear about this book, let's just say, we seemed to tie at every competition. This actually is true BTW. It seemed like in most things we were very evenly matched. I remember arm wrestling challenges that would go for what seemed like 20 or 30 minutes—with neither one of us being able to move the other guy's hand more than an inch or so. We would continue straining to beat each other no matter what it took, or until we were out of the sight of the high school girls, at which point we would both instantly declare "this is ridiculous" and simultaneously release our grips. There is probably a life lesson in that story somewhere, but I should stay focused.

We were alike in so many ways, people often referred to us as twins. But there were two big differences between Dwayne and me. One was that I had a dad at home. In fact, I was the only kid in my neighborhood with a father playing a significant role in his life, much less living under the same roof. Dwayne, like pretty much every other kid in my neighborhood, was being raised by his mom, struggling to get by, and too overwhelmed to exercise much control over what they did or didn't do.

The other difference between us was that I wasn't afraid to try out for sports, so I was on the football team. Looking back at it now, I can kind of see how Dwayne probably wasn't used to having a male tell him what he could and could not do, so following instructions from a coach wasn't really part of his thought process.

> Even in high school Dwayne and I couldn't help competing with each other every chance we got. Scratching that itch provided the setup for one of the most amazing things I ever saw.

Let me explain.

I played wide receiver for our high school football team; it was third string, but that doesn't really matter. The point is, I was crazy fast, there was just a requirement that I also needed to be able to catch the ball at least most of the time, but let's stay focused . . . I was fast! After discovering that I may be one of the faster members on the team, I decided to demonstrate my superiority to Dwayne. And I knew just the place to do it too. See there were two buildings in our school that were connected by a catwalk, a covered bridge that must have been about 120 yards long, basically the length of a football field including both end zones. I bet you see where this is going.

I came up with a devious plan. I would challenge Dwayne to a footrace along the length of that catwalk. I figured for the first 30 to 40 yards I would run fast, but not to my max speed, you know, let him feel good about himself for a minute. Then I would hit him with my cheetah-like prowess, and put it into full gear, like the Black Panther from the *Avengers* movies, even though those movies weren't out yet, but you get what I mean. I would leave him in my dust!

My opportunity came a few days later when we both had somehow managed to *not* find our way to class. (Accidents happen!) We were walking by that catwalk when I sprang my trap. I casually threw out a challenge I knew Dwayne couldn't resist. Dwayne took the bait and I could not wait.

So, we were both at the south end of the catwalk, and my plan was coming together. "On your mark, get set, GO!" We both took off running and I was probably at 75% of my ability and Dwayne was shoulder to shoulder with me on my right. We were about 30 yards into it, so it was time to go Black Panther on him. I looked straight with laser focus at the door, now about 60 yards in front of me, and kicked it into full throttle. Everything went quiet and out of my peripheral I saw wall art on my left side swishing by in a blur. I thought it was odd that I didn't see the same movement from my right peripheral. After adjusting my head ever so slightly in that direction, I saw him. It was Dwayne, and he was somehow still shoulder to shoulder with me. I did not understand. I was for sure at 100%, so I gave it all I had and pushed myself beyond what I could have ever thought was necessary, only to turn to see him right next to me. He looked at me, and in a calm, almost relaxed voice asked, "Are you ready?" Then he just took off and left me. All I saw was the back of his head, and I think I heard a beep-beep sound like the Looney Tunes' Road Runner. He beat me by at least 4 to 6 yards. His speed was ridiculous! I was amazed.

Well, after I recovered from the humiliation, I began to formulate another brilliant plan. I was going to find a way to use Dwayne's superpower to my advantage. You see, there was a somewhat cocky guy in our school who was the star athlete on the track team—the fastest dude on the squad. I'll call him Darrell Jones. (I've changed his name to protect his ego.)

Darrell's track meet times certified him as the second fastest high school sprinter in the entire state of Michigan. I had to see this race happen. I mean, what if Dwayne was actually able to at least keep up with the second fasted high schooler in the state of Michigan? But to make this happen, I had to do a little poking and prodding. It was clear that these guys weren't going to agree to race just to entertain me. So, I slid up to Darrell one day and whispered something like, "Can you believe that Dwayne thinks he can outrun you? I heard him say he'd dust you in a footrace. Can't believe he's disrespecting you like that!" Then I said something similar to Dwayne. Before long, the big race—*Catwalk II, the Sequel*—was on!

At the appointed time, all three of us got lost on the way to class and ended up on that covered bridge. Dwayne and Darrell were on the south end and I was way down at the north end. From that point of view, I could now see that the catwalk had a bit of a hill in the middle; so as they both stood at the other end, I could only see from about the knees up. And when they got into their starting positions, I could only see their heads. Right behind me was a set of metal double doors, the kind with a push bar across the middle and hydraulic closing mechanism on them that closed them slowly so they wouldn't slam.

I was really into my role as the official starter of the race and was being all dramatic about it. Like the starter of a street race with hot rods, as I raised both arms I yelled, "On your mark, get set, Go!" and dropped my arms.

Both of these dudes took off like they were fired out of a cannon. It was crazy how fast they were moving. And to my excitement, Dwayne was actually keeping up with the second fastest high schooler in the state of Michigan! I resigned as official and spontaneously started cheering for Dwayne. "Go, Dwayne, go! Go, Dwayne, Go!" They were neck and neck with about 50 yards to go. My heart was pumping like I was in the race. "Go, Dwayne, go! Go Dwayne, go!" This is where it got amazing. Dwayne turned to Darrell in his calm voice and asked, "Are you ready?" Then, simply took OFF! It looked like Darrell was running in sand. Dwayne pulled so far ahead that he exploded through his hydraulic door, and it was on its way to close by the time Darrell even reached his door.

It was an awesome event to experience. Just pure, unadulterated speed. Mind-blowing athleticism. Yet no one but me (and now Darrell Jones) were really aware of it. But Darrell was probably not going to be telling anyone about it.

Dwayne may be the most amazing natural athlete I've ever seen or known. What amazing gifts God had given him, but those gifts remained unopened. Why? He believes it's because he had no one in his life to encourage him. No one to set boundaries. No one to challenge or steer him.

> Looking back, I now realize that many of the things I resented or found too hard about my earthly father are the very things that allowed me to open the gifts my heavenly Father had deposited in me.

I've kept in touch with my friend over the years, and he seems to still carry some anger and bitterness about that very thing. He believes his father's absence from his life as he was growing up is the main reason he's struggled in life. He points to that void in his life as the reason a guy with his amazing natural gifts hasn't experienced success or achievement.

So strong is that disappointment that to this day when I try to talk to him about the love and guidance of a Father he can't see it, it's hard for him to receive or accept it.

That is so tragic, because the truth is, Dwayne is *still* gifted. And the One who made him is ready and willing to provide all the good things a good father provides, so he can open those gifts for all the world to see.

He is allowing the past absence of a physical dad to keep him from embracing the current presents of his spiritual Father. And that Father will always love and encourage him. The same is true for you and me.

We have to make sure the broken parts of our "horizontal" relationships don't keep us from the vital "vertical" relationship that can bring everything else into order and wholeness.

CHAPTER 3

COME OUT OF THE PIT

The best jokes written are the ones that start with the punchline in mind. He or she knows exactly how the bit will end. There's a *premise*—"Two guys walk into a bar . . ."—and there's a *set up*, but the *punchline* is the destination the comedian has in mind. The order of how the information is shared is deliberate. It's going somewhere.

I've discovered this isn't just true in comedy, it's true in life, too. If you'll live your life with the punchline in mind, you'll live a life of meaning and purpose.

> In other words, when you have a goal, when you know where you are going, every experience becomes a stepping stone and every day becomes valuable.

Your decisions, your actions, your attitude—they are all shaped by the place you want to get to: the punchline.

This is something I've had to learn. I didn't always live with the punchline in mind. In fact, there were many years of my life that could best be described as a monologue of rabbit trails—no real premise, no identifiable set up, and therefore no punchline. I was floating around really in survival mode, just figuring things out as I went. If the song lyrics *"sitting on the dock of the bay wasting time"* hadn't already been written, I would have written them. However, I wouldn't have actually gotten the song published because that would have been a punchline. This is especially true of my teenage years. But as I look back, it's interesting that even during that time, I was learning lessons that were preparing me for my ultimate calling. As a teenager with an understanding of comedic timing and a healthy appetite to please my friends, I wasn't really a stranger to making bold moves to get what I wanted. Now I felt the need to make a bold move in another area of my life—at work—and what a lesson a brother learned.

During my high school years, if you were looking for me on Monday through Saturday between the hours of 4:45 p.m. and 10:00 p.m., Instant Oil Change is where you would find me; more specifically, you'd find me in "the pit." I'd wake up about 6 a.m. to walk to school and be there by 7:50, then I'd go to football practice. After practice, I'd catch two city buses to work and most likely become the greasiest fourteen-year-old probably ever. But it had its perks as I had a Jheri curl at the time and the oil from the pit seemed to work as an activator, however, I smelled like a 4-door Buick.

Now you have to understand, the pit is where I lived after school. I was not permitted to talk to customers, run the register, or even see the light of day. My place was underground, below the cars. We called it "the pit." It was in the pit that I changed oil for every kind of car you can imagine: sedans, minivans, four by fours, hatchbacks, coupes, and Nissan Maximas (they were the worst!)—you name it, I changed it.

It was grueling work for a grown man, let alone a fourteen-year-old. Our shop had the highest volume of any of the stores in America. The oil was hot and the pace was fast. I was allowed only 10 minutes to change the oil and other fluids before I would hear the infamous "ding ding," which meant another car had pulled up. Hour after hour, day after day, I worked in that pit, changing oil as fast as I could.

I've always had a strong work ethic. I mean, as long as I was getting paid more than 60 cents and an orange, I would put my heart and soul into that job. And the more I did it, the faster and more proficient I became. In no time at all, I became the LeBron James of the oil-changing industry, and my co-workers knew it. I was fast as lightning. No over-tightened oil filter could slow me down. Oil plug tightened, differential checked, rubber fitting greased, filter replaced—oil change done! I had all the moves. I'm not saying I was the G.O.A.T. (greatest of all time), but if there was a conversation to be had about a possible Oily MVP, my name would have probably come up, or at least it would have been in the conversation. Michael Jr. . . . World Champion Technician! I can almost see the other employees carrying me off on their shoulders, but I was pretty oily so that may not have ended well.

And that's when it happened.

One day . . . I came out of the pit.

My journey "up top" that day wasn't because I was trying to break the rules or gloat about being ahead of schedule. The reason was simple: I was bored. I had finished the oil changes in all three bays quicker than the guys up top could check the windshield wiper fluid and put air in the tires, so I left the pit to see if I could help. At the time, it didn't seem like a big deal, but that trip out of the pit set me in a whole new direction.

It turns out I was really good at talking with customers. Someone would come in for an oil change, and after I finished changing the oil, I would come up and explain additional maintenance issues their car needed. I wasn't pushy, and I wasn't trying to "up sell" them. I would just politely let them know about other services we offered. And customers responded! In a matter of days, our revenues picked up significantly. It turns out I could do more than just change oil—I could sell. I could negotiate. I could give the customers a great experience.

I was a natural with people, but there were still things I had to learn. For example, I was talking to a customer about rear differential fluid, and I was using language that I grew up using around my friends—"Yo, check it. Here's what you got to do, dog. Every 35,000 miles, this differential fluid got to be changed. Otherwise, the car will start buggin' out."

I remember this old white woman staring at me as she sat in the driver's seat of her car and instinctively hitting her power locks as I spoke, even though her window was down. It was pretty weird, and I took myself right back down into the pit.

Shortly after that incident, the regional manager came down into the pit and explained to me what exactly had taken place. He taught me that when communicating with customers, I had to articulate in a way that they could connect with and receive the information. He went on to explain, "Sometimes you have to meet people where they are to get them to where they need to be." It was a great lesson, and it was his way of encouraging me to come out of the pit and try again. That regional manager was really like a dad to me, and the reason for this is mainly because he was my dad. Michael Sr. was the one who got me the job at age 14, and he would use every opportunity he could to teach me how to navigate life, just like he did from the pit that day, just like he still does today.

About four years later, I was working at an independent oil change location as the assistant manager, when two businessmen came into the shop and spoke with the owner about buying the business, but they had one condition: "If we're going to buy this shop, we have to have an assurance that Michael Jr. is going to stay on as an employee. We need his expertise. He's making $6.75 an hour now. Do you think he'll stay if we raise his pay to $7.00 an hour?"

I overheard the conversation, saw an opportunity, and I pounced. It was clear to see that these guys, with their manicured nails and three-piece suits, knew nothing about changing oil.

When they approached me about staying on and giving me a "raise," I gave a counteroffer: "I'll stay on, but not just as a technician. I would like some ownership."

Because of the understanding I now had about communicating with people where they were as opposed to trying to get them to where I was, I was in a position to actually communicate what I really wanted to see happen. I also understood my value as not just someone who could do a job. I understood my value so much that I was able to negotiate something much better than just more money.

And you know what? They agreed. I became 10% owner of the company with an option for a larger buy later. At 18 years old, I owned my own shop!

As I look back on it now, I realize that interacting with customers in that first oil change shop was some of my best preparation for my career as a comedian. There's not as much difference as you might think. Comedy is about interacting with people, negotiating through conversation, asking them for a response, and giving them a good experience. That's something I could only learn "up top." None of it would have happened if I had been satisfied in the pit.

> Stepping out and trying something new took me from labor to ownership. And I've never forgotten that lesson.

I wonder if you find yourself in your own pit. Have you settled in a place that is safe? You may even be really good at it, but on some level you know it's not satisfying?

Sure, it's convenient to do what you're doing, but is there something in your heart that dreams of more? Of course, it feels safer hiding that talent, but will you ever be really happy if you don't put yourself out there and take a shot? If you've been hurt before, it makes sense if you'd rather not try again, but is that the life you really want to live?

> Whether it's in your career, a relationship, raising your children, or in regard to a talent or dream, as long as you settle for "just good enough," you're spending time in the pit when God has so much more available to you.

He's the One who gave you that gift. He's the One who placed that dream inside of you. He's the One who sparked that idea you have—and He's the One who is calling you up top.

Before I finish this chapter, I have to give you one more detail. It's a pretty important part of the story, because my journey out of the pit didn't come without opposition.

One day, a new assistant manager, who we'll call Mark, got transferred to that first shop I worked at. He was a white guy, maybe twenty-eight years old. He didn't know I was the regional manager's son, and I saw no reason to offer up that info either. Mark was not the nicest person. He would sometimes throw racial slurs at me while I was in the pit. I didn't mention this to my dad because I already knew I was way more important to him than his job position, and also because they didn't call my dad "Big Mike" for nothing. On one occasion, Mark saw me up top talking to a customer and shouted across the shop, "Hey Junior boy, what are you doing up here? Get back in the pit. That's where you belong." Needless to say, I was hurt. As much as I wanted to go off on him, there really wasn't much I could do but head back down into the pit. As I got down into the pit, I heard my dad. He had witnessed the whole thing. "Mark Kowinski, I'd like to speak with you, please," he said in the same tone he would use when I was in trouble, but this time it made me feel safe.

My view in the pit, as I stood under the Honda Accord with the muffler warming the left side of my face, was about 6 inches between the service floor and the bottom frame of the car. All I could see was my dad's black, steal toe, size thirteen boots walking toward the back lunch area with Mark's shiny, new, brown leather, size tens following a few feet behind. I couldn't make out exactly what was being said, but I'll never forget what I saw. As they walked away from the pit area, my dad stopped about three feet from the break area's freshly painted red and grey wall. Mark followed my dad and stopped about two feet away from his boots. From my point of view, all I could see was from their shins down. As they both stood there facing each other, I was trying to make out what's being said, but just then the car motor started up and I couldn't hear a word. Next, there was movement. My dad took a slow step with his right boot toward Mark's left boot and then the same with the other foot. They were now toe to toe, with less than half an inch between their toes. About five seconds passed when I noticed Mark's left foot leave the ground. I assumed it was because he was about to plant it elsewhere so he could walk away. But no. I then saw that Mark's right foot also started to raise up off the ground, and although I could not hear over the shop sounds and the Honda engine, I kind of knew what was being communicated.

This was for sure confirmed moments later when I made my way up from the pit to go to the restroom, and for some miraculous reason, Mark seemed to be trying out for the most helpful guy in the world contest. He was so kind and considerate after his conversation with my dad that it was somewhat awkward.

What my dad later explained to me is important: As much as possible, try to meet people where they are, but sometimes you have to let them know where you're from.

When you step up and step out, there will be days when you face opposition. Not everyone will be happy you're breaking barriers and reaching for your dream.

> But when circumstances come against you, when critics demand you stay in your place, when it feels like taking that risk is too hard, don't give up.

You've got a heavenly Father who stands up for you. He never meant for you to live in the pit. He called you up top for a reason, and most importantly . . . He's got your back.

CHAPTER 4

THE VOICE THAT SAVED MY LIFE WITHOUT SAYING ANYTHING

Comedy is about decisions, judgment calls, and timing. The best comedians can read the response of the crowd and know immediately what to say next. Every decision a comedian makes on stage determines the success of his show. If the timing is off—if miscalculated even the slightest bit—the laughter can quickly turn to awkward nothingness.

But this isn't only true of comedy, this is true in life too. Success in a relationship, a family, or a career is also determined by the choices we make.

> Wise decisions lead to progress and accomplishment, but bad decisions can be devastating.

I saw this firsthand as a teenager. I didn't *always* make the best decisions growing up, but I had a voice in my head in life that kept me from making catastrophically bad choices—it was the voice that belonged to my dad. And it was his voice that saved my life one day.

Before I tell you the story, let me give you a little background. First of all, my dad was one of the only father figures in our neighborhood growing up. There weren't a lot of "dads" around. He was kind of the example of authority for not only me but for other kids on the block too. And my dad didn't play around. He was strict but fair, tough but . . . well . . . just tough. I had a healthy fear of my father. I didn't want to let him down, and I definitely didn't want to get on his bad side.

I remember one time going to my dad and asking him for an expensive pair of tennis shoes. My friend, Demarcus, was sporting a pricey pair of black Reeboks— those things were dope. This was before black tennis shoes were even a thing, and we were all impressed. It seemed like the other kids in the neighborhood were getting all kinds of new stuff, but my dad didn't spend money on stuff like that, and it drove me crazy. I didn't see the wisdom in it at the time; I was just frustrated.

I couldn't help but think, *Even though I'm in high school now, some of my friends are also in high school, and their parents are still buying them stuff. They seem to love their kid, but Dad doesn't hand me anything.*

When I asked my dad about it, he told me, "Michael, unfortunately, you're going to see what will probably happen with those kids one day."

Looking back, I see now that he was talking about the consequences of no discipline in your life and having everything handed to you. But at that time, I just remember thinking, *Yeah, I see what's happening. They're taking up all the popularity and all the girls, that's what's happening.*

When I was sixteen years old, Demarcus came around in a dope new whip (translated: a fancy new car). He was speeding through the neighborhood and showing off his new ride. Now, I knew Demarcus didn't have that kind of money. *How the heck did he get a car, especially a new car like that?!*

I finally caught on to what was happening when he showed up a week later with a different car . . . and then the week after that with yet another new car.

Demarcus was, how can I say this, borrowing these cars from people without them knowing it.

He'd steal a car and drive it around for a few days and ditch it before the police could find him. Then he'd steal another car and do the same thing. This became his regular routine, always one step ahead of the police. And he was getting away with it. I'd be walking to school, on a freezing morning down Kalamazoo Street, and Demarcus would zoom past me with another new car full of girls. When he would see me, he'd stop and say, "Yo, Mike, get in," but I could hear my dad's voice in my head. There was no way I was about to get into that car. So, time after time, day after day, I'd say, "Nah, I'm good, man."

Well, except for one day . . .

Demarcus showed up with two good-looking girls with long hair in a Camaro Z28 Convertible one hot Michigan afternoon—that car was too awesome to resist. When he offered me a ride, I jumped in without thinking. I remember two things about our joy ride that day: 1) I felt scared the whole time, because I just wasn't where I was supposed to be; and, 2) it only takes seconds at 100 miles per hour for the wind to snatch off a girl's hair weave. When he drove me back to my house, I got out of the car knowing that I wouldn't make that mistake again. *My dad would kill me if he knew.*

A few days later, Demarcus showed up with a Pontiac Firebird Trans Am with T-Top and a game plan. He was going to drive to Kalamazoo to pick up some girls, and he wanted me to go with him. He said, "Michael, these girls are fine. You wanna roll?"

Even though I swore to myself just a few days before that I'd never hop into a stolen car with him again, I was so tempted. I leaned hesitantly into the car and thought for a few seconds. On the one hand, Demarcus was my best friend, and this car was so incredible . . . but then I looked down and saw him wearing those black Reeboks. It jarred my memory. I could hear the voice of my father in my head, *Michael, unfortunately, you're going to see what's going to happen to them one day*.

"Nah, man, I'm gonna pass."

That afternoon Demarcus pulled away in that beautiful red Trans Am, and I went in the backyard to pull away at our lawn mower starter rope. It always took like 18 pulls before that thing would start; that day it felt like it took 73. I remember thinking how messed up this was. He was having fun, and I was doing yardwork. He was getting girls, and I was getting grass stains. My life was whack.

That night, when my dad got home from work, he sat down to watch TV, like he always did, while I finished up my chores. When I came into the living room, a story being reported on the local news station sent chills down my spine.

There had been a terrible car accident on the 131 freeway involving a Pontiac Trans Am.

I watched in disbelief as the reporter detailed the single-car accident just outside of Kalamazoo. A red Trans Am had been driving at a high rate of speed and struck a light pole. The driver had been thrown from the vehicle before the car flipped four times and landed on top of him.

The news reporter didn't release a name, but my heart and my mind were racing. *Please don't let it be Demarcus. Please don't be Demarcus. Please don't be . . .*

As the reporter at the scene signed off, saying, "This is Dan Danila reporting to you live from the 131 freeway," the camera zoomed in one last time on the crash scene, and in the center of the screen was a single black Reebok tennis shoe. I could not get my body to move, watching the TV with tears welling up in my eyes. My dad didn't notice at first, but I was overcome with grief. It was all I could do, with tears now running down my face, to turn to my dad and say, "Dad, that's Demarcus." We both immediately ran and jumped in the car to find out what we could do.

Demarcus nearly died that night. His rehabilitation was long and difficult but pretty miraculous. The doctors said he would never talk or walk again. Well, his voice box came back, and he was able to talk. He sounded like a four-year-old girl with an extensive vocabulary for the first month, but he was able to talk. They said he would never walk again. I went to his house to visit him at 4:00 p.m. one day, like I did every day after school, and he wasn't in his bed. I thought, *Oh, no, what happened?* Well, using the walls and the side of the bed, he had walked himself to the bathroom. His recovery was amazing. Everyone, including me, was astonished.

During those long hours by his bedside, I was reminded of how important decisions are. If I had decided to get in the car with him that fateful day, I knew I would have died. The crash was so devastating, there was no way I would have survived it. Even if I had survived, like Demarcus had, what kind of life-altering injuries would I have had?

> And that's when I came to have a new appreciation for my father. It's his wisdom—his influence—that had given me the courage to go back to cutting grass instead of hopping into that Trans Am. His voice had saved my life.

I don't know if you have a father like mine who said the right thing to you even when you didn't want to hear it. Maybe, for you, it's not your dad's voice but the voice of a mother, an aunt, a teacher, a boss, or a pastor. Whoever that person is, be thankful that you've got someone who gives you the wisdom to make better decisions than you might make on your own.

But just as importantly, there is another thing I'd like you to take from this story: *You can be that voice in someone else's life*. You can be the person who gives them a different perspective. You can be the one who warns them not to make the mistakes in life you've made or seen others make. You can be that voice they hear in the back of their head when they're wanting money for expensive tennis shoes or leaning into a Trans Am.

> You can be the voice that
> saves someone's life.

CHAPTER 5

FUNNY THING ABOUT HAVING A GUN TO YOUR HEAD

The year was 1991, and I was working harder than I had ever worked in my life. One of the oil change stations where I was employed throughout my teenage years was about to become mine. Months earlier, I had jumped at a chance to buy the shop and become the new owner. I could imagine the marquee now: *Michael Jr.—Owner, Operator*. It was a dream about to come true.

But just like any dream, it hadn't come easily. Hard work was required, but I was up to the challenge. For months I had been working 84 hours a week to save up the money I needed to buy the shop. My life could be described best by four words: work, eat, sleep, repeat.

Everything I did was about saving the cash needed to become a business owner.

I had my own apartment at the time, but I was rarely there. I would come home each night, exhausted from another 14- or 16-hour day, grab a bite to eat, then fall exhaustedly into bed. And when I say fall, it wasn't a long fall because my bed was a full-size mattress that was about 7 inches thick located in the middle of the floor. I didn't have a TV, table, chairs, and who needs silverware when sporks are free in the drive-thru. The apartment did have an air conditioning unit that did an amazing job of cooling a 5-foot radius. I didn't use it anyway. I had to save every penny I could. And besides, I was rarely at the apartment during this time. I remember thinking that I could furnish the apartment later.

(Picture this: A bare apartment with nothing but a single mattress on the floor and a refrigerator that had some drive-thru condiment packs and half a box of cornmeal. I'm not even sure what happened to the first half.)

They referred to the place I lived as an apartment complex, but to be honest, it wasn't really that complex. There were a few sketchy elements . . . and one lived right across the hall from me. Even though I was hardly there, it wasn't hard to tell that my neighbors across the hall were most likely in the pharmaceutical business. A more direct translation: they were selling drugs. It was pretty clear that the people coming by weren't looking for a Bible study; but because I was never home, I didn't think too much about it. My whole focus was on my work. I was about to become a business owner!

One night when I came home, I saw a gas company van parked near our building. That was weird to me because our utilities were all electric, not gas. It wasn't super hard to figure out that this was the police and they were on some kind of stake out. And when I saw the same van a few nights later, I figured the police must be staking out my neighbors. I just shook my head, thinking, *Man, I'm glad I'm not mixed up in any of that drama. I'm too busy staking out my future.* What I didn't know was that I was about to be collateral damage in the whole thing.

It happened a few nights after I first saw the gas company van. I had worked another 16-hour day, and I was exhausted. It was late when I pulled into my apartment complex parking lot, and immediately I knew something was going down. The van was in the same spot it had always been, but the dome light was on. As I pulled up to the apartment, it clicked off. Out of the corner of my eye, I could see bodies taking cover behind nearby cars and shrubs in front of my building. It was clear to me these were police officers taking cover as I pulled up. I put my car into the parking spot, turned it off, and took a deep breath. As I sat in the car for a few more seconds, it was completely silent, almost too silent; there was zero movement outside.

Having grown up as a black person in Michigan, I knew how I should present myself to police officers. There are lessons we are taught explicitly, and there are other lessons that we learn inherently. I slowly rolled my window down, put my hands out of the car window, and respectfully spoke into the darkness, "Officers, I don't have anything to do with why you are here. I'm just coming home from work."

Nothing. Complete silence.

"I am about to get out of my car slowly."

So, I pulled the outside door handle with my left hand to unlatch the door so it could swing open, and immediately lifted that hand in the air to the same height of my already extended right hand. Using my left leg, I now gently pressed my knee against the door, slowly swinging it open. With both hands still in the air and no one in sight, I turned my hips, then gradually placed my left then my right foot on the pavement. (Why am I giving you so much detail? Because when your heart is racing to the point that you can feel it from the fear of something that is about to happen to you that you can't control, the details seem to get sketched into your memory.) As I shifted my weight to my feet to stand, 10 to 15 police officers descended upon me, yelling orders at the top of their voices.

"Stay right there! Do not move! Keep your hands up! TURN AND FACE THE CAR!!!"

I understood they didn't know who I was, and that they had a job to do, but I was also really scared so I obeyed the orders to a T. With my hands in the air, I once again told the police officers, "Look, I don't have anything to do with why you are here. I don't know those people in my building. I just live here. I'm just coming home from work."

Making sure I was firmly up against the car, they searched me and my car for weapons. Again, I explained, "I'm just coming home from work man." One of the officers asked, "How do we know that?"

"Check my wallet ," I said. "My address is on my ID."

This is when the encounter began to go even further downhill. You see, as I said that, I realized I didn't actually have my ID on me. I had left it in my apartment when I went to work that morning. When they discovered I didn't have any identification on me, the officers started to get even more antsy, and because of this, I felt more unsettled.

"Officers, if you let me walk up to my apartment, as soon as I twist the key to my apartment door that will show you I live here," I said, trying to hide the fear and nervousness I felt. This was starting to get very uncomfortable. I just wanted them to leave me alone so I could get my four hours of sleep and go back to work.

Keep in mind, I'm wearing my uniform from the oil changing shop. I'm covered in oil and grease, and my name is labeled on my chest. What kind of drug dealer wears a name tag?! And if I wasn't a drug dealer, but just some guy showing up to buy drugs, they had already searched my pockets and knew I wasn't carrying any cash. This all seemed pretty whack to me.

Smelling of 10W30 motor oil and apprehension, I slowly walked up to my apartment with about seven officers around me. I nervously put the key into the lock and turned the key, unlocking my apartment door. I'm not sure I had ever been so relieved over something so simple. *Sigh. Relief. This was finally going to be over.* Now they could see that I lived here and was just a guy coming home from work. But I abruptly realized that this ordeal was not even close to being over.

As the door cracked open, the officers aggressively pushed their way into my apartment and began searching all over, I guess to secure the premises. Now, it's at this point in the story I want to remind you how my apartment was furnished—no table, chairs, or furniture, just a single mattress in the middle of the room. It didn't seem funny at the time, but I have to say looking back on it, my apartment kind of resembled a crack house. In their minds, I was probably an oil-changing crack dealer with a lousy air conditioner.

This is where the story takes an ominous turn. With all their attention back on me now, they firmly instructed me to provide identification.

They were more interested in my identification than ever, so I told the officers my ID was in the cabinet above the stove. One officer, who seemed to have a grudge against me, looked down at me as I sat on the floor and said, "You get it." My heart started to race even faster as thoughts ran through my mind, *Why would he have me get it? I'm on the floor. There are plenty of officers already standing in the kitchen. Why is he asking me to do this?* I was just as afraid of his possible reaction if I questioned him, so I carefully got up and walked toward the stove with three or so officers surrounding me. We walked to the cabinet together and I slowly raised my hands reaching for the cabinet to open the door. That's when it happened. I felt the barrel of an officer's revolver press against the back of my head, and felt the vibration of him pulling the hammer back.

I froze, afraid and angry at the same time. I recall one single tear rolled down my cheek. I couldn't believe this was happening. Was I about to die?

I talked the officer through the process with my hands in full view: "I'm reaching for my ID. I'm pulling my hand out slowly, sir. I'm turning around to hand it to you." Now facing the officer with the gun and tears of anger and fear running down my face, I said, "Here is my identification."

With no apology, the officer put his gun away and walked out of my apartment.

The other officers stayed for a little longer, realizing

that I was "Michael from the oil change shop" and not "Big Mike from the Block." The police officers tried to smooth things over, even making little jokes like, "Nice apartment, man." They hung around for another minute or two, making sure I wasn't going to complain to the department or anything like that, and then they left like nothing had just happened.

I remember thinking, *Who can I call? The police???* So, I sat there on my floor in complete disbelief and anger. After being in that state for some time, pondering what just happened and what could have happened, I heard a knock on my door. It was the girlfriend of the drug dealer from across the hall.

I had never met her before, so this was a pretty uncomfortable introduction. She was inconsolable, and I think she mostly spoke Spanish, because I could only make out about every fifth word. The police had arrested her boyfriend and took all of their possessions. She was left with two small kids and didn't know what to do. She cried at the top of her lungs, "They took everything. I don't know what to do. Please help us, please."

It didn't seem like the right time for me to give her a lecture on how to properly choose a boyfriend, and how he was part of the reason I was just almost killed. As weird as it sounds, even now as I write about it, all I really thought about in that moment was how could I help these people.

She felt abandoned, had no money, and seemingly nowhere to turn. Her kids looked hungry, but what could I do, open my refrigerator and offer them a ketchup packet? So, I reached into my wallet and gave her $14 and some change. As she thanked me profusely, with tears still rolling down her face, she gathered her children, and before walking out my apartment door gave me a warm tear-filled hug. As I write this, I have to tell you it wasn't just her eyes that were watery at that moment.

I may have blessed her with all the cash I had on me, but what she gave me was so much more valuable. It was the very thing that I felt was taken from me by the encounter with police moments earlier. I needed to feel needed, like I mattered. I needed to feel like a person again. And that was what this little Hispanic lady with two kids on her hip did for me that day.

It is funny how life works. After this encounter with a lady, whose name I don't know, my anger for the police officers immediately began to subside, making forgiveness for how I was treated a reality down the line.

I believe that anger preserves and intensifies pain or past hurts. The sooner we can let it go, the faster our hearts will heal and grow.

CHAPTER 6

A TRIP TO THE MOVIES THAT CHANGED EVERYTHING

There is something funny about opportunity: you never know when it's going to show up. Opportunity is like that friend that bails on you twenty times in a row and then appears at your house on a random Tuesday night and eats all your food. You didn't know it was going to show up, but you are kind of glad it did.

Opportunity knocked on my door when I was eighteen years old. It was a warm spring night and my friends and I decided to go to the movies. In the middle of the movie, the projector stopped working, causing the entire popcorn-crunching crowd to groan in disapproval. You may have been there before: the movie freezes at the best part . . . the house lights come up . . . everybody turns and stares at the teenager running around frantically behind the projector room glass.

The longer we waited for the projector to be repaired, the more unsettled the crowd became. People became disgruntled and were all about to leave to find entertainment elsewhere. That's when opportunity started knocking, well, more like elbowing.

My friend, a German exchange student from Germany (that's redundant), sitting next to me in the movies jabbed me in my side and said, "I dare you to go down front and tell a joke."

Now, you have to understand, I didn't see myself as an actual comedian. I certainly had no thoughts of doing stand-up comedy one day. In fact, outside of creatively recommending a local optometrist to be the referee at our high school basketball game, I had never done any public speaking before. I was just a regular kid who liked to make his friends laugh.

> But when your friends dare you to do something and you are eighteen years old and without a fully developed frontal cortex (part of the brain), you accept the challenge. And that's exactly what I did.

I got up from my seat and started making my way to the front of the theater. The walk seemed to take place in slow motion, which was a good thing considering the only joke I could think of was a dirty joke, so I had to reconfigure the joke in my head before reaching the stage. Let me explain: See, my cousin and I had a deal that neither of us would swear or use sketchy language. The deal was that if one of us broke the pact, the other could punch the foul-talker as hard as he could right in the chest. My cousin was with me that night . . . I wasn't about to get hit. Plus, I'm trying to entertain the people, not start what would later be known as MMA (Mixed Martial Arts).

So, from the time I left my seat until the time I got to the front of the theater (about twelve seconds), my mind was racing, trying to rework this joke. I understood the timing, the rhythm, the pacing of the joke, I just had to change a few details and land the punchline. This wouldn't be easy, but I felt strangely calm. Like an architect drawing up plans, my mind was drawing up the joke.

I can't tell you exactly what the joke was that night, but I do remember that the crowd roared with laughter. It was mesmerizing. To see people respond that way, to know that I had brought joy, to hear a room full of people, who were upset just moments earlier, now laughing—I had never experienced anything like it. I was hooked.

The movie projector was still under repair, so the audience began to shout, "More! More! Tell another joke!"

But I didn't have any other jokes prepared. So, I slowly panned the audience and did what I knew I had to do, I dropped the mic. I'm just playing . . . I didn't have a microphone, but that would have been really cool. I actually just said the only thing I could think of: "Thank you, folks. Have a good night." Then I exited stage left. The crowd applauded, appreciating the boldness of an eighteen-year-old kid, and I went back to my seat, having completed my dare.

That's when security showed up.

I guess the security team didn't like it that someone had hijacked the crowd's attention, so they found their way to me and my friends in order to escort us from the theater.

I still remember this white lady who stood up and shouted, "If you kick that young man out, I'm leaving too; and I demand my money back." Then these motorcycle guys stood up and said the same thing. Before I knew it, the whole theater was on my side, demanding security leave us alone and drop the matter. After all, what harm had I done? I simply told a joke.

Security quickly dropped the matter, and before long, the movie resumed but I have no idea what happened in the second half of the film. I was so stunned that I just sat in my seat, totally oblivious to the events around me. My mind was racing, replaying the exhilaration of laughter. All I could think was, *That was incredible*.

> That night in the movie theater was the first time I told a joke in public, and it was a night that set me on a whole new path. In retrospect, I can clearly see that this was God giving me a glimpse of what I was called to do.

What actually happened was, there were some people in disarray, and I happened to be there at that time to use this gift that had been given to me to bring those people together in such a way that they decided to do something that was bigger than themselves. You could say that this unscheduled intermission was really an opportunity for me to access my inner mission, which is really about helping people.

You know, as I think back on that night, I realize I didn't go into that theater knowing an opportunity would present itself. I was just a dude who was still trying to find his place in life. My career path looked limited and my future was not certain. All my friends had plans to go to college and pursue particular career goals, but I was just trying to do my best and figure out things as I moved. When people would ask me, "What are you going to do after graduation?" I would say something like, "I don't know. Go home and have lunch probably." Truthfully, I was struggling to find my place in the world. But it all changed in a moment. One new chance, one small opportunity, and a spark was ignited in my soul. A spark that changed my entire outlook and direction.

Opportunity is funny that way. You don't always get advance notice that it's on the way. You could go out for coffee tomorrow and meet the man or woman of your dreams while standing in line. Today, the person who is senior to you at work could leave for another opportunity and recommend you for promotion. Your phone could ring at any moment with exciting news or a big break.

There will always be interruptions that will happen in your life. When those interruptions happen, are you going to be like the rest of the crowd and just murmur and complain, or are you going to look for and seize the opportunity?

> The question isn't, *Will an opportunity present itself?* The question is, *What will you do when it does?*

Are you ready to jump at the chance and take that leap of faith, or will you sit in your seat in fear that things won't work out? I hope my story will be an inspiration to you and something you'll remember the next time an opportunity arises. The next time life throws you something that seems completely unscheduled—your 2 o'clock is a no-show, there is a delay, you lose your job—consider seeing it as an intermission, an opportunity to get clarity on your inner mission.

Go ahead, I dare you.

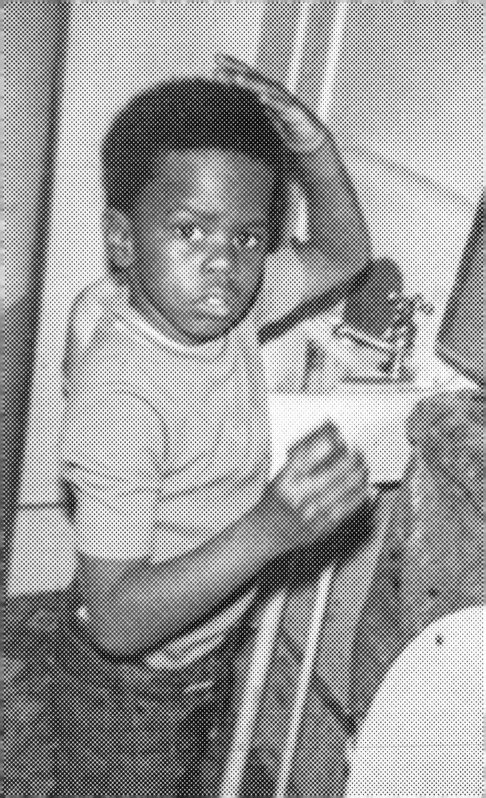

CHAPTER 7

I WASN'T READY TO HEADLINE ... YET

There I was waiting for my invite to be on *The Tonight Show*. I really believed I was ready, even though my comedy career was about an hour and twenty-two minutes old. See, I had just performed my first ever open mic; it was literally my first time performing on stage. And I had smashed it (or so I thought). The next step was obvious I thought . . . *The Tonight Show* on NBC.

As I sat in this now empty comedy club, I recall closing my eyes and thinking to myself: *Just sit tight Michael, you're about to blow up. Any moment a Hollywood producer is going to tap you on the shoulder and enthusiastically ask you to please come share your gift with the rest of the world.*

And then it happened . . . I felt a tap on my shoulder. *Breathe, Michael, breathe. Just be cool and take it all in.* It felt like everything was in slow motion. I turned to see the club manager mouthing words that I couldn't quite hear. *What is he saying? HBO special? Endorsement deal? What?*

"Hey, buddy. We're about to close. Do you have a ride home? What are you doing?"

As disappointed as I was at that moment, it's quite funny now when I look back on it. I assumed everything would happen in my career automatically.

> I thought I was on the fast track; but the truth is, the fast track is rarely the best track.

I wasn't ready for *The Tonight Show* at that point in my life. In fact, I wasn't even ready to headline yet. This is a lesson that I learned over time . . . and a lesson I'm thankful for.

The introduction to the world of stand-up comedy is almost always the same—you start off playing open mics, which normally take place on a Monday or Tuesday night. These are typically not lucrative days for comedy club owners, so they figure the less they can pay for talent the better, even if it means a smaller than normal audience. On top of this, there was most likely a two-drink minimum. So let's recap from the would-be comic's perspective: Your first time on stage is in a room that has a capacity of 200 people but currently has 23; people in the audience paid nothing to get in; and they are probably tired from working another job the day before and have to be up early for work the next day. And with the club's requirement to buy at least two drinks, inebriation is going play a factor in how the audience responds to your untried and true material. If you haven't been to an open mic night before, you really should go. It's bound to be funny one way or another. The talent mostly consists of people who are HILARIOUS . . . at work. But being funny at the water cooler or being the life of the party at a bar is a lot different than performing on stage. However, this is the game, and stage time is what you need to find out if you can work the funny or if you are just funny at work.

For me, I had a hard time getting on stage even for open mic nights. There was only one comedy club in my hometown, and there was for sure more water cooler wannabes than available stage time. But I'm not a person who is easily discouraged, so I started calling clubs in other cities to see if and when they had an open mic night. One guy in Lansing, Michigan, at a place called Connections Comedy Club, told me how the comedy scene there works, and that he was open to giving me a shot but there was a process. He instructed that I had to call their voicemail the Tuesday before open mic night between 9:00–9:30 a.m., leave a message, and someone would call me if I was chosen. Then he said, "Hey kid, if no one calls you, it means you didn't get picked. Don't call the club asking to speak to me. Try again the next week between 9:00–9:30 a.m. If you do get picked at some point, you will have three minutes on stage."

I called that next Tuesday at 8:59. The phone rang and rang and rang. I hung up and called back at 9:03 and got a busy signal. So, I hung up and called back again and got the busy signal yet again. I think it's only right that I pause to explain something for my millennial or younger readers. See a "busy signal" is what you would get if someone called your house phone while you were using it. Now I probably need to explain "house phone," but I don't want to get derailed from the story. Maybe you can research it later . . . look up the word "number sign" while you are at it. (#YouMightBeSurprised) I called every two minutes up to 9:30. I called throughout the day, but the phone just rang and rang. It took about four weeks to get through to an answering machine . . . and the next day I got the call from Simon Cowell saying, "You are going to Hollywood!" Well, I think you get what I'm saying. I got to do my first official performance!

So six days later, I found myself preparing to drive 45 minutes to a city I had never been to; in fact, this was my first time to leave Grand Rapids city limits alone. So I was kind of excited, yet at the same time very nervous—not just because it was going to be my first time at a club, but also because I didn't know if my 1983 Volkswagen Jetta, that had one working door and a decent view through the floorboard that allowed me see the street passing under me, could handle the trip. I had never even dared to try going 55mph before, let alone for 45 minutes. This was a risky trip to do three minutes of comedy and for sure not exactly a sound financial decision, but I was determined, and sometimes determination and a little bit of ignorance are all you need.

I made it to the club and recall watching the other comedians who went on before me. Some of them were okay. I could see how nervous some were. Watching them perform first actually built up my confidence, because I could see what the audience was seemingly rooting for in each performer. It gave me a chance to see how the crowd was reacting, what was working, and what was wasn't. I remember thinking to myself: *I think I could do this. I belong here.*

Six of us got stage time that night. I was fifth on the list. The first guy was kind of funny. He wasn't fall off your chair funny, but he held his own. The audience seemed to be just tolerating the next two guys and giving a few chuckles here and there. But everything changed with the fourth guy—this dude was eating it. It was brutal. The only ones suffering more than him was the crowd. It was cringeworthy. As he made his way off stage seemingly having no idea how poorly he had performed, he motioned to give me a high five. I didn't know if the unfunny was contagious or not so I opted out of the high five and just gave him the best "let's not make this awkward" smile I could give.

When I went on the stage that first night, I still remember what it felt like. It's hard to explain, but it was like time slowed down while it was speeding up. I was very nervous and strangely confident at the same time. I still remember my first joke . . .

We're going to have fun tonight. We're going to laugh. Better not nobody heckle me, because the last person who heckled me, I hit 'em in the jaw. I punched him in the stomach. And then I grabbed him by the back of his wheelchair and pushed him outta my way.

You have to remember, I only had three minutes, so I was hoping I could cram all my jokes in because it was such a short amount of time. I did my whole set, and when I was done with every joke I had written, I had 1:42 left.

I ran out of material.

I got off the stage, the emcee was scrambling, but still I felt good about my set. It was some okay funny stuff. It just went too quickly. I had a lot to learn. That first night was the night I thought I was on my way. I was so sure that someone in the crowd would see me and invite me to play *The Tonight Show*. As I mentioned before, that didn't happen. Instead of an invite to be on television, I got an invite to see if my car would start back up so I could head back to Grand Rapids.

Comedy takes time.

My initial "success" led to more open mic nights, and eventually, I was asked to emcee. That's a big deal—it's certainly a step up from the open mic. The emcee gig was a good spot for me. First of all, it paid a whole lot more, well, at least enough to get three-fourths of my tank filled with gas, but also because nobody expects the emcee to be funny. Your job is to keep the show rolling; and if you're funny, that's a bonus. I loved bringing "bonus" laughter. I didn't know it at the time, but during those nights as an emcee, I was growing stronger as a comedian. I was learning to be funny on the fly. It wasn't always about a list of jokes. It was more about reading the room and responding to the crowd. This was a lesson that would come to be an important part of my act down the road.

I had moved from an open-mic-wannabe to a club emcee. But all the while, my dream was to headline my own show . . . and that chance would come sooner than I thought.

My emcee success led to the next step for a comedian—to feature. A feature act is one step below a headliner. The feature comedian goes on about 30 minutes before the headliner and warms up the crowd. Finally, my hometown comedy club, The Comedy Den, asked me to feature. Keep in mind, years before I couldn't even get three minutes on an open mic, but now I was the featured comedian. This was huge.

I featured at The Comedy Den and apparently nailed it. It went so well that I started getting invitations to feature all over Michigan and, of course, I jumped *at* the chance. Being the feature act meant that I could now afford a half bag of groceries and a full tank of gas! For the next several months, while holding down a full-time job, I traveled all over the state, featuring in every club I could. But it was one night outside of Detroit that surprised even myself.

I was playing at an A Room called Mark Ridley's Comedy Castle. (An A Room is the best spot to play. A B Room is a pretty good opportunity. And a C Room just means "you need to get outta here before it gets dark.") My show went so well that night at Mark Ridley's Comedy Castle that they had me come back on a regular basis. I was smashing it!

One night after I featured, the owner, Mark Ridley, pulled me aside and said, "Hey, before you leave, I want to go ahead and book you again, but this time I want you to headline."

This was huge. I was blown back. Headlining was everything I had been working toward. I'm thinking this was one step short of television. To headline would mean my name would be on the marquee. People would actually be paying money to come see me. I could probably afford to buy some tuna to go on the tuna sandwiches I had been eating. This was every comedian's dream.

I'll never forget that moment. There I was, standing in the hallway, surrounded by the photographs of all the famous comedians who had headlined at Mark Ridley's Comedy Castle, realizing the fulfillment of all I had worked for, and I heard myself say . . . "Mark, I don't think I'm ready."

Mark was shocked, but he wasn't the only one; I was having an internal argument with myself as well. We are talking about real tuna from the can. Mark had never had anyone turn down the headlining position, but I knew I wasn't quite there yet. I still had work to do, and I somehow knew if I accepted that invitation, I would be taking a short cut that would hurt me in the long run.

> I tell you that story because . . . sometimes I think we are so anxious to get to a destination that we overlook the importance of the process.

That might be in your career, in a relationship, in the pursuit of a dream, in the way you're raising your kids—sometimes we come to resent the process rather than appreciate all that it is teaching us. Those nights on an open mic, those sets as an emcee, the stopping at every other highway rest area to have a conversation with my car about why it was important that we press on— they were all teaching me lessons I desperately needed to learn. I had come to appreciate the lesson instead of resenting it. And when Mark approached me about headlining, as badly as I wanted this opportunity and some protein, I knew I had a few more lessons to learn.

What lessons are you learning on your journey? Are you allowing yourself to adjust and mature? If you were short-tempered before, are you learning to keep your cool? If you were judgmental and critical before, have you learned to see people in a different light? If you were impulsive and unwise in your past, have you learned from your mistakes and become wiser and more thoughtful?

I ask for a reason. You see, if I had started headlining before I was ready, I would have failed. It actually would have set me back in my career, not move me forward. And the same is true for you. If you don't learn the lessons from the journey, you'll go backward instead of forward.

Thankfully, the end of this part of my story worked out pretty well for me. I took another nine months as a featured comedian. I used those nine months to refine my set, improve my skills, and learn from other headliners. Eventually, my set became so strong that headliners didn't want to follow me. I was getting bigger laughs than they were, and clubs wouldn't let me come as a feature—it was time to headline.

But I don't know if that would have ever happened if I had jumped at the first offer that came my way. I wasn't quite ready at the time, and impatience would have stunted my comedy, not propelled it.

Featuring was a checkpoint for me. I had to pass that checkpoint before I could headline effectively.

> We all have checkpoints in life—personally and professionally. And we can't go to the next levels until we pass the checkpoints along the way.

I remember early in my marriage my wife and I were trying to refinance our house in hopes to not lose it to foreclosure, but we were having a problem qualifying for a loan. The broker came to me with a shortcut to cheat the system. He said, "Hey, man, all you have to do is list your wife as your agent so it will look like you have two incomes." But the problem was that my wife wasn't my agent. I told him that I wasn't comfortable doing that and it didn't feel right. He told me, "You're going to lose your house if you don't do this." But even with that threat and the fact that we had four kids, it wasn't something we could do.

The broker called back a couple of days later and said, "You're not going to believe this, but a program just came across my desk that you qualify for. You're going to get the house at an even lower interest rate than what I could find before!"

You see, that was a checkpoint for us. It was almost like a test. We had to pass the integrity checkpoint in order for us to find a new level of success.

What about you? What are your checkpoints? If you'll be patient, you can use your current experiences to learn and develop in your relationships, your career, and in your soul. Are you ready to wait a little while longer so you can learn a little more?

Trust someone who has been there—if you can be patient, you will be headlining and enjoying a tuna melt before you know it.

CHAPTER 8

MEATBALL SUBS AND MY FOUR-DOOR APARTMENT

Have you seen the *Mission Impossible* movies? They are awesome. Tom Cruise can find his way into anywhere he wants with the greatest of ease. But I think the story would play out differently if he was a newbie comedian trying to break into a New York City comedy club.

Yes, you have to be good. But lots of really good comedians never break through. Sure, you have to stick with it. But some hang in there for years and years and never get their break. *Dang, Michael Jr.,* you may be thinking, *it sounds like it would take some sort of divine intervention for you to get your break.* Now you're starting to understand.

As you already know, my journey in New York City got off to a rough start. A few months into my time there, I was really struggling. I hadn't run out of heart or desire, but I had quickly run out of cash. It wasn't long before I found myself living in my car with all of my belongings, including my previously borrowed Marriott comforter. (Note: I actually did return that comforter to Marriott.)

Speaking of covers . . . I did my best to cover up the fact that I was living in my car. This may sound kind of strange, but I was never really one to try and flat out lie to people. So I would sometimes try to park on the east side of the street, that way if someone happened to ask where I lived, I could truthfully say, "I live on the east side." And if necessary, I'd say my address was 1997 Lumina Drive," because my car was a 1997 Chevy Lumina.

Now, I was at least fortunate enough to get stage time at some of the B and C level comedy clubs in New York, but they paid like $8 to $12 for the night, and there was little chance of an A Room booking agent seeing me there. This being the case, I had to be super careful of how I spent what I had. My food budget basically allowed me to buy one five-dollar meatball sub sandwich per day. Trying to get on stage at comedy clubs meant staying out really late at night. One way I would compensate for the lack of food was by sleeping as late as I could. Breaking the mode of what you may think about comedian types, my default time to rise had always been around 6 a.m., but

I figured it best to wake up as late as possible, basically having sleep for breakfast. So I would try to stay asleep in my car at least until 11 a.m., depending on parking enforcement. After waking up and figuring out a shower plan, it was off to Subway to get a footlong meatball sub for five dollars. I'd cut that sub in two pieces, eat the first half sometime in the afternoon, and then, no matter how hungry I got, try to wait until around 9:00 p.m. to eat the second half. It was a balancing act between my economics and E. coli food poisoning.

Some of the clubs would provide free coffee and stale popcorn at the bar. So on those nights, I could eat the second half of my sub sooner and fill up on popcorn and coffee later.

I had been in New York for about four months, was out of money, sleeping in my car, and had made it onto a real comedy club stage only a handful of times, and only for a few minutes each time. I knew that to turn things around, if not financially at least emotionally, I needed to find a way to get on stage at one of New York's top clubs. This would be a huge morale boost. So, I set my sights on the world-famous New York Comic Strip Live Comedy Club. All the great comics worked that stage in their early days coming up. Getting on that stage could, if you were really good, be a stepping stone to bigger things and better days. I knew it would be hard; this iconic room was on Manhattan's Upper East Side, but

I figured I might have a chance seeing how I was also from the east side.

Of course, every struggling comic in the city and probably the country knew of the Comic Strip and would do whatever it took to get along with the club's manager and booking agent in hopes to get more stage time there. Which made getting on that stage as an unknown very hard. How hard? Harder than me coming up with a hillbilly saying people sometime use to express how hard something is. Anyways, at the time there were only two viable ways for an unknown to possibly be seen by the club's manager. One was to do a bringer show or do the open mic night. Neither of which was very easy to pull off. A bringer show is where a wannabe comedian can do five minutes on stage if he brings at least eight friends who pay to get in and those eight friends pay for at least two drinks each. The problem with this is, I didn't have eight friends in New York who would buy a ticket to see me. I actually didn't even have eight friends. The other option was a Tuesday night open mic.

But to get on stage on one of those nights began by doing 90 seconds of your material in front of the club's manager. If, and only if, he really liked you, you *might* get scheduled to appear on a Tuesday night a week or so later. As a result, the line to do your 90 seconds for the manager started forming around 6:00 a.m. and usually stretched halfway around the building.

I jumped through all of the hoops and somehow got scheduled for an open mic night, but I wasn't in the clear yet. There was always a danger of getting bumped off the schedule if some famous comedian dropped into the club and was willing to do an impromptu set or was wanting to test drive some new material.

Finally, my big night arrived. I, like every other aspiring comic scheduled to perform that night, was incredibly nervous. Just as my time slot was approaching, I saw him walk into the club. My heart sank as every head in the place whipped around to get a peek. George Wallace, the well-known comedian, not the dead governor from Alabama, was in the house.

The moment I saw him, I expected the worst. I was only minutes from finally taking my place on that stage, and I was sure that I was about to be bumped. Bumped as in he was going to go on before me and do as much time as he wanted, and if there is any time left or air in the audience members' lungs, then I might get to go on. My worst fears were only confirmed when I saw the club manager head my way after talking with Wallace. I braced myself for bad news.

Instead, I experienced a clear instance of that divine intervention I mentioned above.

The manager said, "Hey, George is going to do a set. Do you want to go on before him or right after him?" I was stunned. This never happens; I'm not supposed to get an option here. *What?* Attempting to hide my bewilderment, I told the manager I would like to go on before him. And that's what I did.

My set went really great. The audience laughed. Hard. The manager laughed. And, as I would soon find out, George Wallace laughed too.

Later, a cluster of my fellow young comics were standing around George asking him questions. But after a minute, he spotted me, left them, and headed my way. The next words I heard were, "Hey Michael Jr., you're really funny. And unlike most of the new guys these days, you're clean. So, let me ask you, why don't you swear in your act?"

I knew I couldn't tell him the real reason, which was I didn't want to get hit in the chest by my fourteen year old cousin, which, as I thought about it, didn't make sense seeing how I was now a grown man. So I gave him a partial reason that might also break the ice; I shrugged and said, "I don't know. What if my grandmother decided to skip church, catch a flight, and walk into the comedy club?"

To my relief, he seemed satisfied with my answer. So, the next thing I heard was this: "Well, I like your act and the fact that you are clean. I'd like you to come do a show with me and my best friend." Now, I cannot explain how awesome this was. I was so pumped! So excited! I was going to be doing a real comedy show with George Wallace and his best friend, whoever he was.

George called me the following Monday to give me the address to where the show would be. It was a place called Rascals Comedy Club in West Orange, New Jersey. I tried to sound cool over the phone as I sat at my dining room table (open glove compartment) with a meatball sub on it, "Cool man, see you then." I hung up the phone so pumped I went into the den (passenger back seat) and did a little dance.

Then I had a thought that needed my attention. So, I went for a walk and then to my office (driver's side) to do some math. George Wallace never mentioned if it would be a paid spot, and I didn't dare ask him. I mean, I couldn't. It was such an honor, any comic would do it for free in a heartbeat. But the reality was, I had about $31.68 to my name. I'd be able to get three more meatball subs to last me through Thursday and put $10 of gas in my apartment (car). This would leave $6 to last me until I did a spot I had booked at a one-nighter in the city that would pay about $20. Seemed like a good plan to me. Then it hit me. If I left New York City to get to New Jersey I'd be cool, but there was a toll cost of $8 to get back into New York. If the George Wallace show didn't pay, I wouldn't be able to get back. I don't know why my first thought after coming to this realization was, *What if they don't have meatball subs in New Jersey?* So, I did the only thing that made sense on that Thursday night: I headed to Rascals Comedy Club to meet George Wallace.

I walked up to the door and the bouncer looked like he wanted to practice his bouncing skills on me. In a voice that seemed to be making his gold chain vibrate, he asked, "Can I help you?" I was like, "I'm a comedian. Michael is my name, Michael Jr." He was like, "Oh yeah, Wallace said you would be coming through." He unfolded his arms, opened the door and said, "Head this way, dog." There was something bigger than I can explain about this interaction.

As I walked into this club, it was as if everything was in slow motion. Then I was a surprised by something so amazing words can't explain it. It almost brought tears to my eyes to experience it. It was the smell of freshly cooked food!

The place was full of comedy fans ordering food, awaiting the show to start. As I neared the greenroom, I looked forward to talking with George Wallace and meeting whoever his best friend was. When I entered the greenroom, I connected eyes with George and a big smile came across his face. Then as I panned the room, there he was; his best friend was none other than Jerry Seinfeld. This was pretty doggone cool. Now I'm not really a fan boy by any means, but I've always had the utmost respect for Jerry's ability to deliver the funny.

The guy sleeping at 1997 Lumina Drive and living on subdivided meatball sandwiches found himself opening for George Wallace and Jerry Seinfeld! I crushed it, too. We did two shows that night and I got two standing ovations.

> None of that happened without the help of a heavenly Father, one I didn't even know about. But my heavenly Father wasn't finished intervening.

I stayed at the club long after the crowd was gone, partly because I wanted to soak up as much as I could of what just happened, including the smell of cooked food. And the other part was because, in the back of my mind, I thought when I walked out of that club I had no idea what I was going to do; I only had $5.46 to my name. The club was pretty much empty—no comedians, nor audience members, just a few waitresses. So, I quickly realized I am borderline loitering at this point and that I should leave. As I headed back up the stairs, the manager called my name, "Michael Jr." I turned as he walked toward me; my heart was racing, and I'm thinking, *Is he about to give me $20 for the set I did? Wait, I did two sets. Is he going to hand me $40?* I think I could feel my heart beating faster as he opened his mouth and asked, "Hey, would you like to go to church with me tomorrow?" I was like, "What? Huh? What did you say? Church?" In a fraction of a second, I was taken back to when I was seven years old, when my grandmother would take me to a place called "church" that lasted what seemed like 11 hours, where a guy up front would yell as he tried to get the phlegm out of his throat at the end of each sentence. I looked at the manager and was like, "No man, I'm good. Thanks for asking." I decided to hit the restroom before leaving because the one in my apartment didn't exist. As I walked out of the restroom, a very beautiful, almost mesmerizing woman said to me, "Oh, hello Michael. Great comedy set tonight. I'm Kim, Phil's fiancée, the manager. Did you get a chance to talk to him?" I, unknowing at the time, just kind of kept staring at her. As I snapped out of the short trance, I could hear her saying, "Would you like to go to church with us?" Still kind of gazing at her I said, "Absolutely! I've been trying to find a church for a while now." She gave me the address on a napkin.

For a moment I thought to myself, *I actually could use a church or something right now*. Then I looked at the napkin and it was a New York address and the reality of my situation came crashing back down on me. I didn't have enough money to get back into New York, and I didn't know how to get to the eastside of New Jersey. I said my goodbyes and headed out the door. I was full-on overwhelmed as I headed to my car. I had just had maybe the greatest set of my comedy career, yet it looked like it was all about to end. I literally didn't know where to go from there. Then the big bouncer dude from earlier called me, "Hey, Mike Jr.?" "Yeah," I said as I walked closer to him. Then I said, "Thanks for having me here man," as we both instinctively slapped hands to shake and gave each other a half hug. In an instant I noticed that the hand slap wasn't as loud or crisp as I expected. I quickly realized this was due to what felt like some paper in his hand that he was now transferring to mine in the beats of our embrace. As I exhaled I could tell it was cash, and I was so excited I almost started to cry, but that would have been weird because we were still making eye contact. This had to be the $20 or $40 for the set I did. Of course, I didn't want to look in my hand right then, but we both played it cool. He said, "George Wallace said to give you a little something something." I was like, "Cool," while stepping backwards, trying to maintain my composure. "Thanks, Bro."

I remember opening my car with my left hand because I didn't want to open the other hand until I was sitting down. As I sat there with my fist on my right thigh, I could feel that it was two bills for sure. I would be grateful for whatever; two tens would be great, two twenties, would be amazing. For whatever reason, I tried to open my hand one finger at a time. Pointer, then middle, then thumb, and then as I pulled back the remaining fingers, my vision started to water as I looked down in silence. The next sound I heard was two tears crashing onto the surface of two crisp hundred dollar bills.

I just sat there for ten minutes in awe of what had just happened.

> Now with puffy eyes from wiping tears, I glanced over to the passenger seat and noticed the napkin with an address written on it. The next thought I had was one I had not ever had before: *I'd like to go to church.*

Now to be real with you, I thought church was only for weird people. I had heard a few Christians tell their stories about how they were near death and found Jesus. (I now know these are called "testimonies.") Or how they were addicted to drugs or alcohol and Jesus saved them. I figured, *I'm not dying, an alcoholic, or a drug addict. I don't smoke. I don't even curse! So why am I thinking about this?*

Up to that point, I'd only encountered weird Christians. At least that's what I thought. Having lived a little more, I now understand that most Christians are very unweird, but there always seems to be a creepy person in every kind of group, kind of like just about every family reunion has that one uncle. So, if you're a Christian reading this and you're saying to yourself, "That's not true! No one in my group is creepy or weird," it's probably because it's you. I just hope you are not also that uncle!

The next day I found myself at the Christian Cultural Center in Brooklyn and my experience that day was not anything like I expected. After some cool music, this guy came up and started talking about Jesus like a normal person. He wasn't ranting and raving or calling down fire on sinners. He wasn't wearing a shiny suit or sporting a fresh, tight perm. Instead of running around waving his arms and sweating, he just calmly and clearly explained about who Jesus was and what He came to do in a way that I could understand.

At the end, he gave what I now know to be an "altar call." He explained that entering into a relationship with God was as simple as believing in my heart and confessing with my mouth that Jesus died to save me, and that He was raised from the dead.

I wish I could tell you that I responded right then and there. I certainly wanted to. But I thought that before I bought the merchandise, I should probably read the brochure. I decided I was going to read the Bible . . . all of it . . . before making a decision about becoming a Christian. Now, I struggled with reading as a child, which we'll get to in a later chapter. I don't really like reading. (Which makes it a little ironic that you're sitting here right now reading a book I wrote. Enjoy!)

So, my decision to read the Bible was no small thing. And the first challenge I had to overcome was, well, I didn't have a Bible. Later, I was walking through a convenience store when some random woman walks up to me, hands me a Bible, and then walks off without saying a word. Yeah, kinda like in a movie when the hero blows up a car or building and the explosion is behind them but they don't flinch or even look back—yeah, like that. Boom! Problem solved!

So, I dove in. I started on the very first page, which turned out to be the copyright page. There I saw that the Bible was made in Grand Rapids, Michigan. I thought, *Wow, me too. That's my hometown. Wonder why we hadn't met before?* So, I just jumped in. Now being honest with you, even though I'm 26 years old at this point, I had never read a book from front to back before, and didn't know if the Bible was an autobiography or a story book. So, I just started at the beginning, which was awesome because that is what it actually said, "In the beginning," then I just kept going.

Over the next several weeks I spent every waking hour either doing stand-up in clubs, attending church, or reading the Bible. I'd often read for fourteen or fifteen hours a day. I eventually made my way to the New Testament, where I encountered the gospels for the very first time. I read through Matthew and toward the end, came to the part where Jesus was arrested in a garden, gets killed, and then was resurrected. This blew me away. I didn't know that Jesus died for me until that very moment when I read it in Matthew. I really didn't know. Yes, I had been to church before, but I just didn't understand until that moment, and I was like, *Wow.* Then I turned to the book of Mark and Jesus died again. I was really tripping when

I got to the book of Luke and He started heading for that garden a third time. I'm yelling at the pages, "Don't go in there Jesus! It's a trap! How can you not know this by now?" Then I got to John. Same thing! Hand on my heart, I literally thought Jesus got killed four times.

After 36 days, I'd read the entire Bible, cover to cover. I didn't understand a lot of what I'd read. But I'd done it. And I wanted to give my life to Him more than ever. After meeting the Father who created me, I learned that I was no accident.

> I came to understand that my ability to make people laugh was no accident, and I am to use this gift for something much bigger than just me. I discovered then and now know that I am funny for a *reason*.

Looking back, it's clear to see God's fingerprints all over my story. When we take time to look back and notice what He has done, it makes it so much easier to trust what He is about to do.

CHAPTER 9

THE TONIGHT SHOW PICKED ME

Success is when opportunity meets preparation.
–Zig Ziglar

This has been true in my life as a comedian, and it's true for you, too—*whatever* your career or personal goals. And trust me when I tell you, there will always be opportunities. It may seem like you've been waiting for a long time, but keep in mind, opportunity shows up when you least expect it. It's not a Facebook Event that comes with advance notice and 137 people clicking "Interested."

> Opportunity is sneakier than that. You have to be ready and prepared in advance so when the moment comes, you can seize your opportunity.

This is what happened for me. This is how I got on *The Tonight Show* the first time.

I had been living in New York for a few months, trying to get any stage time I could. I really liked New York. It was hard work, but the people were great, and I was working on my act constantly. I was a young comedian in the Big Apple, just hangin' and chillin'. And by "hangin' and chillin'," I mean I was broke and pretty much homeless. And when I say, "pretty much homeless," I mean actually homeless. About a third of my time in New York City, I lived in my car. So, it wasn't easy . . . but I used every moment to prepare for any opportunities that could help me get what I had been dreaming about.

I started to feel it was time to move to Los Angeles. You ever get a feeling of spiritual clarity where you know it's the right thing to do? Well that's not what I had. I had $142 to my name with no New York income opportunities in sight. My stomach was most of the time empty and I had a gas tank to match it. My choices where pretty much "give up on my career and head back to Michigan with my tail between my legs," or "see if I can somehow make it to Los Angeles where my cousin had a couch I was welcome to," which sounded so much better than my current routine of rationing gasoline between driving and turning the engine on for nine minutes every sixty-five minutes to stay warm at night.

After another divine intervention, I made it to Los Angeles. Now Los Angeles has, in my opinion, the number one comedy club in the country. It's called The Comedy & Magic Club in Hermosa Beach. This club is so prestigious, I couldn't even get *inside* much less get time on stage. But this is when my preparation in New York started paying off. You see, when I met comedian George Wallace in New York, he told me, "If you ever need anything from me, give me a call." So now, here I was in LA, thinking about taking him up on that offer. I wasn't able to get into The Comedy & Magic Club on my own. I needed someone like George Wallace to get me access.

Here's the crazy thing: I didn't even have to call him . . . he called me! And he called me with an opportunity; "Hey, you want to go to The Comedy & Magic Club with me?" I was blown back! I should have played it cool, but there was nothing cool about my answer. After I picked myself up off the ground, stopped crying, and caught my breath, I said, "Sure, man, why not?"

We showed up at the club together and it was so awesome, but I could feel, for whatever reason, that I would not be getting on stage that night. I could have been impatient and disappointed, but remember what I said earlier, opportunity sneaks up on you. It doesn't always look like what you expect . . . sometimes it's much better.

George Wallace looked at me and said, "Hey, follow me." This is where things got, as I would describe, "even more ridiculous." He took me backstage and into the greenroom. WOW times eight.

So, here I am in the greenroom, not only with George Wallace, but also in the company of comedy legends, Gary Shandling and Jay Leno—the Mount Rushmore of comedy . . . and me. There was so much knowledge in the room to absorb, and I was very hungry; but not just for the knowledge, I was literally just hungry. See, I hadn't really eaten that day and only had $11.64 to my name. Even though they made it clear that I was welcome to any of the spread of food that was laid in front of me on the buffet, and I really wanted some of the delicious looking chicken wings that seemed to be calling my name, I opted to only reach for about three french fries. I suppose I did this for two reasons: I didn't want to come across as the starving artist that I literally was, and I didn't really feel great about taking their food without having something to give. So, as I casually chewed on the delightfully crispy fries, they started back in on a joke they were working on for Jay Leno's *Tonight Show* monologue. I just listened politely, trying not to be overwhelmed by the fact that a food other than ramen noodles was entering my digestive system. The subject of the joke was about a football player who was suing the NFL for 400 million dollars. Apparently, an official had hit a player in the face with a penalty flag, and the player had lost vision in one eye as a result.

They were pitching jokes back and forth to each other and then, oddly enough, the room grew quiet as they looked to me. After taking a half a bite of french fry number three, I looked around the room with my heart kind of racing and somehow calmly untethered these words, "Okay, let me see if I got this right. He got hit in the eye with a flag. He lost his vision in one eye, and now he's suing the league for 400 million dollars? He's not gonna see half of it." BOOM, the whole room broke out in laughter. I took it all in for a few seconds and then grabbed three chicken wings.

One of the things I learned from this moment is that your gift will make room for you.

I also learned the importance of preparation. All those shows in New York, all the practice in front of a mirror, all the hours spent writing jokes in my car and on my cousin's couch paid off.

About a month later, the owner of the club, a great dude named Mike Lacy, called me up and said, "*The Tonight Show* is down here auditioning guys for their upcoming live show that's going to be via satellite from the Montreal Comedy Festival. Why don't you come down and do your set?"

Obviously, I couldn't get there fast enough. When I arrived, there were 10 comedians set to go on—I was number 11—but *The Tonight Show* was only going to choose one person. You could feel the nerves in the greenroom, and *nobody* wanted to go on first. The reason you don't want to go first is because if you're first, you don't have the chance to read the room. You'd rather someone else do it, so you can see what the audience is like that night and get a feel for the room and what they are responding to.

As I was sitting there listening to all the comics come up with very creative reasons why they shouldn't go up first, I thought to myself, *You know what? I'll go on first.* And before I could think about this thought, I said it out loud. So I went on first. After the night was over, the producer came up to me to talk, and at the end of our short conversation, he looked me in my eyes and said, "Hey, we want you. You're the one." Wow! I felt like the character Negro from *The Matrix*. (I'm sorry I misspelled his name, but it's kind of funny so I'm going to leave it.) The point is, they picked me and I was going to be on *The Tonight Show* on NBC!

I'll probably never forget the experience. What made it even more memorable was that it was live. See, all late-night talk shows, including *The Tonight Show*, are pre-taped, but this was the first time they had a satellite show from the Montreal Comedy Festival, and they wanted to do it live. The pressure was incredible. I mean, if I walked on stage and fell on my face, the whole country would see it on live television. If I stumbled on a joke or got heckled by the crowd, the whole country would see it in real time. I am grateful that didn't happen. I did my set and smashed it! It felt awesome. Everyone commented on how smooth and cool I looked on stage, and I felt great.

While I was in the Montreal greenroom exhaling for the first time after saying "Hi" to the live audience, *The Tonight Show* producer came up and said something I'll never forget: "Michael, I have to be real with you. When you went up on stage that night at the comedy club to audition, I was actually irritated because I hadn't heard of you before and I didn't want to waste my time. I just wanted to see my top three guys and go home." Then he said, "But I had to watch you because you went up first, and obviously I was impressed as was this audience here tonight, and *that's* the reason you got on *The Tonight Show*."

As I write about that incredible experience, I'm reminded of the gifts that lies within all of us. You may not realize it, but you have a gift inside of you. No matter your age, your past disappointments, your perceived limitations—you have been given the ability to do something great. But sometimes, in order to see that and really utilize your gift, you have to be ready to jump at the opportunities that present themselves. That means allowing yourself to be uncomfortable and not shrinking back when you feel uncertain. I was "uncomfortable," and I felt "uncertain" when none of the other comedians volunteered to go first at the audition, but opportunity isn't always comfortable. Of course, I was afraid, but I wasn't going to let that fear keep me from jumping. I had to have faith and be willing to go for it.

> If you look back on your life, I think you'll see that God has been teaching you, molding you, preparing you for the purpose He has for you.

It probably hasn't always been easy. Maybe you've had some bad sets or slept on your cousin's couch, but it has all been preparing you for something better. Always remember: You have been given an amazing gift, and it will make room for you.

CHAPTER 10

THE HYSTERICAL JOKE THAT WASN'T FUNNY

Comedians see funny in everything. It's just the way we're wired. We can take even the most traumatic experiences and turn them into comedy gold. Because that is my perspective,

> I've come to discover that everything we go through in life can be used for something good—nothing is wasted.

You may not see it at the time, but your setback can be used as a setup for your punchline.

This has certainly been true in my life. It was a pretty significant setback that helped me write a joke I did the first time I played *The Tonight Show*. Jay Leno called it a classic. The joke went something like this . . .

> *I was on an evening jog in Beverly Hills recently when something strange happened. While I was jogging, this white lady, who was also jogging, turned the corner ahead of me onto the same street I was on. She was jogging probably 30 feet in front of me, heading in the same direction I was.*
>
> *I saw her glance backwards over her shoulder and immediately sped up. It was almost like she was afraid. I didn't know what was behind us, but if a white lady was afraid of it, I was afraid too, so I started jogging faster.*
>
> *Then, she looked back again. Now she looked terrified, and she busted out in a full-out sprint. I thought,* Oh, snap. Someone is after us. *And I started sprinting too. Me and this white lady must be in trouble.*

(By now, the audience gets where the joke is headed, and the laughter keeps growing.)

I didn't want to pass this lady up and leave her to the boogeyman behind us, but her sprint wasn't fast enough. We weren't going to survive the mugging, or whatever we were running from, at this rate. So, I yelled out as loud as I could, "Hey, lady, is that as fast as you can run?"

The audience is falling out at this point. I didn't even have to explain that the white lady was running from me the whole time. It was a successful joke that effectively shed light on issues of race and stereotypes without being preachy.

After my set, as I mentioned before, Jay Leno told me that joke was a classic. He couldn't stop laughing. It was nice getting that compliment from *The Tonight Show* host, but what neither Jay nor the 12 million viewers who tuned in that night knew was that joke had its roots in a very true story for me—quite a painful story.

I still remember it vividly. I was seventeen years old and fishing with my dad at Reed's Lake in East Grand Rapids, Michigan. East Grand Rapids and Grand Rapids were two very different places at the time. East Grand Rapids was an affluent area with beautiful homes and high-income earners. Grand Rapids . . . yeah, not so much. Comparing East Grand Rapids to Grand Rapids isn't necessarily like comparing Beverly Hills to South Central Los Angeles, but you get the picture.

Anyway, after a day of fishing, my dad and I brought the boat up to the dock, and he instructed me to go get the truck and trailer and drive them back to the dock. I started on my half-mile walk to the truck, but it was getting dark and cold, so I began to jog. It was about this time when . . . you guessed it . . . a white lady who was out for a jog, turned the corner ahead of me, jogging in the same direction.

Yep, it really happened.

Just like in the joke, she looked back, saw me, and began to sprint. But a funny thing happens when you look backward and try to run forward—you lose your balance. And just like in a scary movie, this white lady fell down.

In her panic, she tripped over the edge of the grass and hit the sidewalk.

At this point, I'm not even thinking that she was running from me. It all happened so fast, the thought never occurred to me. All I knew was that this lady was running, looked back, and fell down. So, naturally, I ran over to help her.

You have to understand the way I was raised. I was taught not to ignore someone who was hurting, especially a woman. For my whole life, it had been ingrained in me to help a person who was in distress. I think that's a pretty reasonable thing to teach your children. If someone is in trouble, you stop and help them. It's really that simple.

But as I ran over to help this lady, she began to scream. I didn't understand at first what was happening. Why was she screaming? She fell down and I was going to help her. But it quickly dawned on me that she was screaming because she was afraid of . . . me. We had never met. She didn't know anything about me except for what I looked like, but that was enough to frighten her.

I wanted to calm her fears and explain that I was trying to help her. I could see she was in distress from her fall; and because of my upbringing, I was anxious to help. But the closer I got, the more she panicked.

There is another part of this story I forgot to mention—there is an East Grand Rapids Police Station right across the street from the spot where this lady had fallen. My instincts quickly told me that if the police came out, heard this lady screaming, and saw me standing there . . . it wasn't going to be good for me. So, as I looked her in the eye, I went against everything I believed in and ran off. I felt overwhelmingly conflicted with every stride.

I got to my dad's truck and sat in the driver's seat with tears in my eyes. I was upset, angry, hurt, frustrated, and confused all at the same time. At that moment, there was nothing funny about the situation. I had no idea this would one day turn into laughter I would give to millions. All I knew was how much it hurt.

After I took 10 or 15 minutes to compose myself, I finally went and picked up my dad and loaded the boat onto the trailer. I think he could tell I was upset, but he didn't ask me what had happened. We drove home in silence that night.

You know, I didn't tell anyone about what happened that night for almost two years? I just couldn't bring myself to talk about it. It was just too upsetting.

But one night, a year-and-a-half later, I finally brought the subject up of what happened that summer in East Grand Rapids to a friend of mine.

> As I told the story, something healthy for me happened: I started to see it differently. I started to notice the funny in the scenario: *That white lady was afraid of me and I was afraid of the situation.*

Even though at the time I was visibly shaken, looking at it all these months later, I actually started to see the potential funny in the situation.

My setback had become a part of my setup that would turn into a punchline.

When I tell this story to people, there are two things I like to communicate. First, if you've been hurt in some way or you have had something dramatic that happened in your past, a big thing to do in order to start the healing process is to say it out loud.

When you talk to others about it, you will be able to shed some light on it and see it from a different perspective. It might not be funny to you, that's just what happened for me as a comedian, but you will be able to look at it from a different vantage point. Even if you're just talking to yourself, or writing it down, when you communicate the truth of the pain, you will break down those walls and let the healing process begin.

The second thing I want you to see is this: Your setback is part of your set up so you can deliver the punchline you're called to deliver. In fact, it's like a sling shot or bow and arrow—the further you've been set back, the further you're going to reach. You just have to know what you're called to aim for.

> Trauma, disappointment, injustice—these can all be things you use to better yourself . . . and even help other people.

Millions of people have heard my joke about jogging behind a white lady. I've told that story in countless venues, and even made a YouTube video to keep so others can share and learn from it. It has brought incredible laughter and thoughtful introspection to individuals all around the world. What was once seen as a setback is now part of my setup and has literally become a punchline I get to deliver.

What about you? Is there a setback that has held you back too long? Is there a story you've kept hidden that you need to share?

If you take the steps to break down those walls, I believe there will be strength and healing in it for you.

> **Someone out there needs to hear your story, and you need to let it out.**

You may not end up on *The Tonight Show* but sharing it could turn out to be a truly classic moment for you and maybe someone else too.

CHICAGO

LOS ANGELES

CHAPTER 11

OUT OF GAS

One of the first things you learn in comedy is that you never know what can happen. From night to night, show to show, anything can go down; everything can change. Expecting the unexpected becomes the norm.

I think this is true in life, too.

> In the pursuit of your dreams, random, unexpected things can come along at just the right time to give you the push you need exactly when you need it.

This is why it's so important that you never give up. The unexpected can happen at any moment. It's funny how life works that way.

I experienced this firsthand one week in Chicago. It is one of the most pivotal moments in my career. Definitely, a make or break moment for me. The story goes like this . . .

Like many of the comedy clubs I appeared in back in those early years, Zanies in Chicago wasn't a lot to look at from the outside—or the inside for that matter. Just a little hole-in-the-wall place on a narrow side street several blocks north of Chicago's famous Miracle Mile, in an area known as "Old Town." (It came by that name honestly. It was a town and it was definitely old.)

But just because Zanies didn't look like much, doesn't mean the place wasn't significant and considered an A Room. Since its founding back in the 70s, many of the biggest names in comedy have held a microphone on that stage. Jay Leno once called it, "The perfect comedy club." And for reasons you're about to discover, it will always hold a special place in my heart.

My final few months in New York City had been spent living in my car and hoarding every last penny I could scrape together. Why? Because I had a booking at Zanies in Chicago coming up, and I had to have enough gas money to get there. Once there, I hoped to somehow make enough to continue on to Los Angeles, the "promised land" of success and significance in the world of comedy. Because I was living in my car, instead of trying to pay for a room, I was able to stack about $175 by the time my Chicago gig approached. The other great thing about this gig, aside from making some much needed money, was I would not have to live in my car for my time at Zanies. You see, the club had a "Comedy Condo," which sounds fancy, but it's really just an apartment the club has the comics stay in during the week they perform. This way they can save money and not pay for hotel rooms. Comedy condos are never much to look at and on top of this, for whatever reason, each comic that stayed there felt obligated to leave some sort of super-inappropriate prank or practical joke for the next person staying there. I'll spare you the details, just trust me on this: If you're ever staying in the Comedy Condo and you find food left behind in the refrigerator . . . Do. Not. Eat. It. I was just excited about sleeping in a bed that did not have a seatbelt that poked me in my ribs throughout the night.

The reality of my situation is that a new comic just didn't get paid very much. That's why, to help supplement my income, I counted on selling t-shirts after my shows. You can't live on selling t-shirts, but every extra dollar mattered. Up to that point, on average, I'd sold two shirts per show at the premium price of $10 per shirt. This helped put gas in the car, but $10 a shirt wasn't going to get me to Los Angeles.

By the time I arrived in Chicago, gas and food expenses had shortened my cash stack down to about $40. However, seeing that the brakes on my car had been grinding for the final 50 miles or so of the trip, I also had to figure out a way to get them repaired. The repair shop said it would cost $400. I figured if I could just get $250, I could buy the parts and fix them myself behind the club. So, I had to ask the club manager if he would mind paying me the $375 for my performance in advance and he agreed. Now, I did enjoy math in school, especially when things added up, but as I quickly found out, that wasn't going to be the case here. With the advance I got from the club and after repairing the breaks on my car, I had about $160 to my name. I figured if I was able to press in and sell two shirts each day for all six days, this would give me a total of about $285 to work with. This was assuming I would mostly eat bar olives and popcorn and hope that a waitress messed up on a food order—bingo/jackpot! A gallon of gas was around $2.80. I had to travel about 2028 miles and my car got about 14 miles to the gallon. I figured if I didn't spend any money on food or run my heater at night to stay warm and have zero car issues along the way, I would still be $120 or 602 miles short from making it to California.

> You ever get to a place where you unknowingly start to justify not moving forward toward your dreams? I started having those almost subconscious thoughts about how just going back home to Grand Rapids could be the best move to make.

I noticed I was having thoughts like, *I haven't seen my parents in a while, and I kind of miss them. I wonder if the comedy club in Grand Rapids would let me be a weekly emcee? It's not really that bad of a C Room. I bet I could be an assistant manager at the instant oil change and stack enough money to move to California and even have my own place in no time.* Now I know myself well enough to know that if I went back to Grand Rapids the chances of me reaching my dreams were going to plummet, but I didn't know what else to do.

My only other possible source of additional income was those t-shirts. It was all about the shirts. I figured if I could somehow sell enough extra shirts, this would not only be enough money for me to take the risk of driving across the country, but would quite possibly be a sign from God. And I was fully committed to do whatever I thought He would have me do, even if it meant going back home. But, I had this feeling He wanted me to press on, and the only way I could see this being possible was by selling every shirt I had.

Now I have to be honest with you, I hated pitching them from the stage. HATED it. Holding up those shirts and talking them up at the end of a great set just didn't feel right to me. It was like suddenly going from *The Tonight Show* on NBC to a 3 a.m. infomercial pitchman in less than five seconds—"But that's not all, if you act now . . .". But I didn't feel like I had any choices in Chicago; I had to do my part and hope for the best.

In the first five nights of my six-night stand, I managed to sell four shirts and I was pretty discouraged. I only had the Sunday night show left and it was typically the smallest crowd by far, probably because people had to head to their jobs the next day, and I was starting to think I might need to as well. The club held about 120 people. When I walked in the door the emcee was already on stage and there were 27 people in attendance. This was by far the smallest audience of the week. On top of that, none of them were even seated in the first five rows. It was not ideal for comedy by any means. The closer the crowd, the better the jokes hit. The farther they are, the easier the comic is to ignore.

I stepped on the stage that night and brought the best show I could possibly muster. I'd like to say it's because I am a showman and that no matter how defeated I am feeling on the inside "the show must go on," but that's not really it. And it certainly wasn't because I somehow believed that if my jokes were strong enough, I could sell my remaining shirts to a crowd of 27 people. No, looking back at it, I think the reason the show was so strong was because on some level I knew that this could be it for my comedy career. Although Zanies didn't look like much, it was certainly an A Room and quite possibly the last one I'd ever play. The great news is, the audience loved my show. I'd say even though there were only 27 people, it was my favorite crowd by far. So much so I was thinking to myself on stage, *Thank you God for giving me this. Lots of comics don't make it this far and get to enjoy this. I am truly grateful.*

As I finish up the last joke before my closing, the euphoria quickly dropped as I realized I now needed to pitch the t-shirts. I glanced at the one I had folded on the stool and thought to myself, *I don't want to do this. We have been having such a great time. I can probably make it to Grand Rapids with the cash that I have. Why am I doing this?* So, I reluctantly picked the t-shirt up. It was an all-black shirt with my logo and my name on it in white. There was really not much to these shirts at all; I could only afford the one print color. So, I started in on my pitch and I could feel the energy in the room nosedive. I'm sure my new demeaner probably didn't help. So, as I held the shirt up and was about to tell them it was $10, I got heckled by some lone drunk guy: "How much for that ugly shirt?" As a comedian, I knew I'd have to come back with something sharp and quick. So, I settled on a dry stare and the words, "Fifty dollars, dude," and stared at him for two beats. It for sure had to be the timing and the facial expression because the other 26 people cracked up laughing. I then went into my big closing joke, said good night, and reluctantly headed to my spot to sell the t-shirts.

As usual, some people scurried out the door right past me, avoiding eye contact and sometimes mumbling standard compliments to cut through the awkwardness of the moment. Then a cheery white lady approached the table, looked me directly in my eyes, and said, "I'd like one of your shirts please." She then placed a bill on the table, looked me in my eye again, and said, "You are so worth it" and walked off. I thought that exchange was a little different, but I didn't think much about it. I was just happy to sell a shirt and have the ten dollars. Only as I looked down at the table, I saw she actually paid $50. My heart and mind started to race to try and make sense of what just happened. *Was this a mistake? Was this what she meant by "you are worth it"? I need to go catch her. Where did she go?* As these thoughts and more were flying through my head, I was snapped out of it by a man's voice, "Excuse me. Could I get two size large please?" "Sure," I said with my mind still on the lady before him. Then I handed him the shirts, and he handed me a $100 bill, smiled at me, and walked off. The only way to explain what I was feeling at that moment was completely overwhelmed. What has just happened? Now standing there trying to hold in my emotions, a black couple walked up and bought two size small shirts and handed me another $100 bill. I'm still amazed even now. At the end of the night I sold 13 shirts for $50 each. My eyes are watering even as I write this. I recall sitting in my car after the show and just weeping over what had just taken place. I know like I know this was God's way of saying, "Just trust Me. I got you. Now go to Los Angeles."

With that additional $650, I was able to do exactly that. I made it to my cousin's couch in Los Angeles where me and my comforter would crash while I found my way in the new city. I knew there might be more challenges ahead but . . .

> . . . I wasn't afraid to move forward because I knew for sure that God would be with me like He had always been, even when I didn't know it.

Just like He is always there for you, even if you are not aware of it. You just need to seek Him, and I am positive you will find Him. Who knows, you could be just a gas tank away from reaching your dreams.

CHAPTER 12

THE UNEXPECTED RESPONSE TO A RACIST HECKLER

"When are you going pro?" This is a question that exceptional amateur athletes are asked *all* the time. In college, and even in high school, if you can throw it 60 yards, if you can hit the game winning three, if you can bomb it over the fence, the questions start early: "Yo, you're talented. When you goin' pro?"

I remember the first time someone asked me that question. It wasn't related to sports, though. It was about my life as a comedian.

The story starts back in 1999. Comedy wasn't my career yet. It was still just a dream. I was desperate for stage time, and I set my sights on *The Super Show* in Flint, Michigan.

Now, there are two things you need to know: 1) *The Super Show* was a talent show that drew a crowd of over 3,000 "flintstones." That is what the people in Flint called themselves at the time. 2) These flintstones had a Yabba-dabba-doo time booing anyone they could clear off the stage. This crowd was notorious for helping the "talented" rethink their career. They booed people at any opportunity. As if that wasn't scary enough for a would-be performer, Flint, Michigan was the murder capital of the country . . . and they were proud of that fact. So, it's safe to say that was a tough room. It was like the Apollo Theater without metal detectors. And they didn't discriminate; they booed adults, black people, and white people. There were small children in tap shoes running off the stage in tears. The boos rained down just for the fun of it.

So, there I was backstage, more than nervous and feeling pretty doggone scared. I'm maybe the fourteenth person on the list; and because the audience was so ruthless with the boos, performers were cutting their acts super short, if they had the courage to go out on stage at all.

There was a pretty little 8-year-old girl named Tiffany who was going to do a dance number, and then me. I was clearly afraid, and I heard her say, "I can't do it, Mommy. I don't want to go out there, I'm afraid."

That's all I needed to hear. Something seemed to well up inside me, kind of like the Christmas cartoon

"The Grinch" when his heart grew ten times with love. I told her mom that I would go. When I did this, I felt like Superman. Then as I turned, peeking out the curtain at the crowd, it was clear they were kryptonite. Fear jumped all over me but I had to go out there, and I instinctively knew that I could not look afraid.

When I walked to the microphone, before I could even start my set, some dude yelled out, "You better be funny, *#&!*#!*." The pressure was on! I instinctively knew I only had about four seconds to respond with something funny or the boos were going to drop ferociously. So I said, "I just got heckled by the darkest dude in the room. You're so dark-skinned, I bet if you rode a motorcycle, you'd get a ticket for tinted windows." Boom! The place exploded in laughter. It was on and popping from there. I finished my whole set to rolls of laughter.

I walked off the stage that day riding high, knowing I had done more than survive *The Super Show*, I had made 3,000 people laugh. That's when I got the question. Some guy backstage came up and asked, "Hey, man, you got skills. You funny. When are you going to be a professional?"

That's a great question. I had to think about it. Police officers get a badge and start walking the beat. Doctors get a degree and start . . . um . . . doctoring on people. When would I know I was a pro? Was it when I made a certain amount of money? Was it when I headlined a certain club? Did I need a business card to be a pro? I wasn't really sure of the answer . . . but I am now.

Fast forward a few years after the 1999 *Super Show*. Somehow the planet had survived Y2K, and we were all still alive. I was playing this club in the great metropolis of Fort Wayne, Indiana. I wasn't headlining yet. I was just a featured act at a spot called *Snickerz Comedy Club*. That's when it happened. I got the worst heckle of my life.

Every comedian deals with hecklers, but this night was different. What made this guy's alcohol-induced comment so difficult to deal with was that it was racist in nature. He wasn't attacking my act; he was attacking anyone who looked like me. It was a defining moment.

The crowd was mostly white (again, Fort Wayne, Indiana), and I was about ten minutes into my set when some guy yelled from the back of the room with the thickest twang you can imagine: "Michael Jr., I was wondering why all black people look alike!"

The audience froze.

Like I said, this wasn't your average heckle. It was pretty evil in nature.

It felt like time stopped as the crowd stared at me uncomfortably, wondering how I would respond. Would I call for security to have him removed? Would I walk off stage? Would I throw a chair? Would I call Al Sharpton?

Well, I didn't do any of those things. Without even thinking, almost instinctually, I said, "Excuse me, sir, but we don't all look alike. You've just gotta cut the eye holes in your sheet a lot bigger."

The audience exploded in laughter. It was so loud, it almost startled me. And, believe it or not, the guy who made the comment from the back of the room actually stood up on his chair and gave me a standing ovation with the rest of the room. It turned out to be an amazing experience. I shut down the worst heckler of my life, and it was at that moment I realized that I was a professional.

> I've found that in life most of us consider ourselves amateurs. We wonder if we'll ever make it to that "next level." Success seems like a distant goal.

When will I become the kind of parent I want to be? When will I be the kind of spouse I know I can be? When will I have the confidence to stop second guessing myself at work? When will I be happy with how far I've come instead of frustrated with how far I still have to go?

I think the answer comes when you learn to silence the hecklers in your life. A heckler is someone, or something, that tries to shake your confidence and get you off track. For the comedian, a heckler is a rude patron in the back of the room, but the hecklers in your life come in all shapes and forms.

That past failure that makes you second guess every decision you make—that's a heckler. That person who told you that you'd never make it—that's a heckler. That financial obstacle that has you frozen in fear—that's a heckler. And guess what? Even your own voice, that feeling of self-doubt in your own soul—that's a heckler.

Any voice that tries to deter you from what you're called to do is a heckler. And you're going to have them. In fact, if you don't have any hecklers, you're probably doing something wrong. The fact that you have a heckler can be viewed as confirmation that you're moving in the right direction.

> **Never allow the heckler's voice to determine your choice.**

You can't dwell on that mistake. You can't obsess about that doubt. Instead, you've got to be steadfast and know your worth. You have to press on toward the mark. You've got to address the heckler. This may look like you talking to yourself in the mirror, using encouraging words that counter the heckler's. I prefer the Word of God for this personally, as it works every time, or talk to someone who can encourage you. Whatever the approach, you must shut the heckler down and press on. When you do, then you are ready to move to that next level in life. It doesn't make you perfect or pain free; it just means you're a professional.

CHAPTER 13

MY BIG BREAK

I've always enjoyed bringing laughter to people, from the time I was a little boy and even when I started my stand-up career. Being around people and finding the right words to make whatever the current situation is even better is an amazing tool, and I am appreciative of this gift. It's these most recent years that I have really enjoyed the most. My sense of satisfaction, purpose, and real joy in my career are off the charts right now. And it all started with a shift in my perspective. I had a revelation one night, minutes before I went on stage . . . and it changed everything for me.

I usually say a prayer before I stand up to perform. It's not a ritual, and it's not for "good luck," it's just how I get down. (translation: "just something that I do.")

> One night, when I prayed before taking the stage, I remember having this thought: *Instead of trying to* GET *laughs from these people, I should just* GIVE *them an opportunity to laugh.*

Now, that was a thought I had never had before, and for some reason it just felt right. You have to understand, comedy is an aggressive profession. We're all about "getting laughs" or "making people laugh." So, the idea of *giving* instead of *getting* is what I would now describe as a game-changing revelation.

That night, I instinctively moved slower, but I would say it was actually more purposeful. The following is not the best example unless you are a fireman: It's kind of like trying to save a cat out of a tree; you have to be smooth in your approach, no sudden movements, or you could scare the cat. I told you this wasn't the best example. Why would a fireman even save a cat from a tree? It's a cat. I'm sure it can get down. My point is, instead of just jumping right into my act, I just relaxed and interacted with the crowd. I didn't tell a joke right out of the gate. I worked to get a sense of the people in the audience a little before going into the material. I thought of it this way: If you have a gift for someone, you don't show up at their house and give it to them the second they open the door. No, you wait a minute. You come into the house, you say hello to everybody, you interact a little . . . and then, when the time is right, you present the gift. That's what I did that night, and it was incredible. In fact, it was this experience—this shift in my comedy—that helped me write this joke that I like to begin my set with sometimes.

I'll stand in front of an audience for a few beats without saying a word, and then utter something like the following:

> Listen, the jokes are not going to start right away. See for me, comedy is like dating someone you really like; and I really like you guys, but I don't want to rush things. I'm sure you've had other comedians come in and out of your life before. I want this to be different.

This always seems to get a nice laugh and set the tone, but more importantly, it seems to connect us as people, not just as a crowd and a performer but as people.

After I had this change in perspective, I was leaving The Comedy and Magic Club after having a really strong set. I was signing autographs, people wanted photos, we were all smiling and laughing outside the doors of the club, and for some reason I happened to look across the street and saw a homeless man. Now, I had played this club many times but had never seen a homeless person in this area before. I don't think it was because he wasn't there before; I think I couldn't see him before now because I was asking a different question.

I remember thinking, *How could I give someone like him an opportunity to laugh?* It was kind of a passing thought as I assumed it wouldn't work, so I just shook it off. But for the next several days, I kept coming back to this idea that I'd like to figure out a way to do comedy for homeless people.

Well, like four days later, I was doing a fundraising event in the Los Angeles area and a woman came up to me after the show. She said, "Michael, I work at a homeless shelter. Have you ever considered doing comedy for homeless people?" I'd like to tell you that at that very second, I stuck my chest out, found the nearest phone booth, and re-emerged with a silver microphone and a cape. But hearing someone else say out loud "homeless and comedy" in the same sentence, I froze up and said, "Naw, not really, not so much." So, I just took her business card, and a few days later with my legs between my tail (that's not a typo, I just like to be different), I said to her, "Let's do it." What originally started off as a question was about to become a reality. I was going to be able to test this whole "give laughs" instead of "get laughs" on the toughest stage I've been on.

I'll never forget pulling up to the homeless shelter on Skid Row, Los Angeles. Skid Row was a five-block radius that was populated by thousands of homeless people. The air was thick with despair and desperation. I remember seeing an elderly lady eating oatmeal out of a shoe! *What was I thinking when I agreed to do my act here? How could I do jokes in the middle of so much pain and sorrow?* Filled with hesitation, I remembered the question I asked that got me this far, "How can I give them an opportunity to laugh?" So, I just kept walking toward the location.

The homeless shelter didn't have much of a stage. In fact, there was nothing about it that was set up for a comedy show. I guess that made sense, considering they had never hosted one before. I stepped up on stage and dove right into my material . . . but no one was laughing. There were 70 or 80 people there, but no one was even slightly amused at my tried-and-true material. And it was not going well at all . . . or was it? It hit me just then that the only reason I was thinking it was going poorly was because I was still measuring by how much laughter I could GET instead of recognizing that I wasn't accomplishing what I came to give, an opportunity to laugh.

Immediately, it felt like someone removed two bowling balls from my pockets. (I was going to say back pockets, but that's a weird visual.) And suddenly I could better connect with the audience, and I believe at that moment, they were able to connect with me. That's when it hit me: These people weren't here to see comedy; they were here to get a meal!

Now, this next part of the story, some of you will think isn't nice or that it it's in some way insensitive. Because you were not in that room with us on that July evening you may not even understand, but I am going to share with you exactly what happened next because it fully connected us all, and we had an amazing, joy-filled time.

See, I realized that the meal was scheduled to be served at 4 p.m. and it was currently 3:45 and that food, based off the looks I got from people as they would walk in, didn't get served until the presentation was done. After confirming this out loud with an audience member, I said to them, "Well you guys should probably start laughing pretty quick." Then I started my next sentence at just 10 percent of my regular speed, "Two . . . guys . . . walk . . . into . . . a . . . bar . . ." And the place exploded in laughter. Not because they were threatened but because I took the time to recognize what was really going on. We went on and laughed for the next 12 minutes, then shared a meal together after. This experience was the catalyst for the nonprofit I founded called Funny For the Forgotten, where we make laughter commonplace in uncommon places. (BTW: If you want to help us continue in this mission, go to *funnyfortheforgotten.com* and give.)

I share this story for two reasons: one, because it's a book and that's what you are supposed to do; and the second reason is to set up a question I want to ask you.

What question are you asking yourself when you are at work, or with your friends, coworkers, spouse, kids, neighbor, church, clients, or mailman? (Okay, maybe not your mailman, but you get my point, right?)

Are you asking, "What can I give?" Or, are you asking the default question, "What can I get?" If you don't choose which of these questions to ask, you will by nature ask, "What can I get?" When you make the decision to change your question, I guarantee you will find some much better answers.

CHAPTER 14

FOUR $20 BOOKS
FOR $16,000

There are times in life when everybody has to step out of their comfort zone. Professionals, stay-at-home moms, high school students, business owners, retail workers . . . and comedians. It's not easy to do, but what I've discovered is that . . .

> . . . some of the greatest things in life happen outside of our comfort zones.

A good example of this is the $20 children's books that sold for $16,000.

I was doing an event in Toronto. This wasn't a regular comedy show; it was a fundraising gala where all proceeds were going to a local homeless shelter that was doing incredible things in the community. When I got the invitation to do my comedy act as part of this event, I couldn't resist. I may be more comfortable in the ghetto than at a gala, but it was such an important cause that I jumped at the chance to be a part of the night.

I was scheduled to be the closing act of the night. Before I went on, while I was prepping in the greenroom, the organizers did their fundraising thing. I had no idea if it was a success or not, but all in all, it seemed like the night was going well. When they called my name, I stepped out onto the stage of a huge concert hall. The men were all in tuxedos and the ladies were wearing beautiful ball gowns—it was a pretty impressive sight.

I did my act that night to a standing ovation. It was a huge hit. Comedy is really about timing, including the timing of when to get off the stage; so, after getting a thunderous standing ovation from these 2,000 people, I exited stage left. Great night, wonderful people, a funny set, now let's go home.

There was only one problem . . . I felt like there was something I needed to go back on stage and do. I needed to start a different kind of fundraising campaign.

> I sometimes think that when you have that feeling that you should do something to help someone, you should do it within the first ten seconds, or you may think yourself out of doing it.

I struggled with the idea of going back out on stage after such a powerful ending. This was fully outside of my comfort zone: I didn't even know how much money had already been raised. I didn't know how to be an auctioneer. And I had no idea what exactly to say. I'm thinking, *These people are ready to leave. These tuxes probably need to be returned soon. They have babysitters who probably have school in the morning. Now, because of me, instead of being accepted to Yale, it's junior college for her. I can't do this to Amy.* That's right. I'm having all these thoughts about three seconds after having the initial thought of doing something nice for the organizers and the shelter. All my regular instincts said to let it go, but I just had this feeling that my night wasn't over.

So not knowing how I would be received, I walked back onto the stage just as the emcee for the evening was about to dismiss the crowd. Surprised, she said, "Oh, Michael Jr. is back. Everybody, give it up!"

I took the microphone, acknowledged the crowd, took a deep breath, and said, "Hey, everybody, I don't know exactly what's going on or why I should do this, but I feel like I should auction off one of my children's books for this amazing cause. Yeah, that's what I feel like I should do."

I started the bidding at $100. It quickly rose higher—$200, $500, $1,000, $1,200. Between each new bid, I was cracking jokes and having a good time with the audience. The laughter was contagious, and the new bids were rolling in: $1,500 . . . $1,800 . . . $2,000 . . .

I was so excited when we reached our top bid—$4,000! The place went crazy! I felt so relieved that we raised some more money and that the crowd had a great experience, but if I'm being honest, I was equally glad I didn't crash and burn. The risk had paid off, now I could go home.

Except . . .

As I reached to put the microphone back on the stand, I had that feeling again, that same prompting. I wasn't able to escape back into my comfort zone yet; I felt led to keep going.

After standing there for a few seconds that felt like a lifetime, I raised the microphone to my mouth and said, "You're not going to believe this, but I have a question for you. Who else wants to give $4,000 for a children's book?"

Keep in mind, these books were $20 in the lobby. I even told the crowd that. What I actually said was, "Who else wants to give $4,000 for a twenty-dollar children's book?"

Which is both crazy and funny in retrospect. The crowd was totally into it.

A lady in the top right balcony stood up at the exact same time as a guy in the back left of the room, who had dropped out of the bidding for the initial book at $3,000. They both said in unison, "I'll buy a children's book for $4,000." The audience erupted in laughter and cheers. And just like that, we had auctioned off three children's books for a total of $12,000. I was blown away! What a night!

The crowd gave me another standing ovation, which was pretty cool because that wasn't really the point. I think the crowd was just appreciative that I had stepped out of my comfort zone and helped raise more money for the homeless shelter. I started to jog off the stage, feeling like the night had been a huge success, and then it happened again . . . I had that same feeling. *Go back out there.*

At this point, I'm thinking this is ridiculous. I'm a professional comedian. I know what happens when someone stays on stage too long, and that was definitely the risk I was taking. Going back out there one more time wasn't just leaving my comfort zone, it was obliterating it . . . but I went out anyway.

I walked back on stage with my shoulders slumped and the crowd erupted in applause. They knew the night wasn't over, and to my surprise, they were fully into it. I took the microphone from the emcee to tell them again what was on my heart, but an elderly man in the fourth row quietly stood up. His presence seemed to capture everyone's attention. "Young man," he said to me, "I would like to buy one of those twenty-dollar children's books for $4,000." The crowd again erupted in applause, but this time it felt different. It felt like they were not applauding me or even for the $16,000 we had just raised. If felt like we were all applauding each other, because together we did something that made no sense to any of us on paper but made full sense to us all in our hearts.

In just a matter of minutes, we had raised $16,000 for four copies of a $20 children's book.

I found out later from the event organizers that their goal for the evening had been $50,000. Before I went back out on stage, they had raised $35,000—still a lot of money, but far short of their goal. I didn't know any of that at the time. I was just being obedient to what I felt God had prompted me to do. With the additional $16,000 we raised, they finished the night with a total of $51,000 raised to help shelter the homeless.

Had I stayed in my comfort zone, I would have given the people what they wanted from my act—laughs—but what we want and what we need are two different things. They wanted to be entertained, but we needed to be a part of something special, and that's exactly what happened.

> I've learned that comedy isn't really the destination, sometimes it's just the vehicle.

I have two questions for you as you read this book: Did you pay $4,000 for this book? If so, that's awesome. Thanks for the money. I'm sure I used it well. When was the last time you stepped out of your comfort zone? Maybe you're a businessman, but you feel led to volunteer at a local youth program. Perhaps you're a grandparent, but you have a desire to go back to school. Maybe you've spent your life behind the scenes, but you're feeling a prompting to take the microphone.

I don't know exactly what your comfort zone is, but I can tell you that good things happen when you step out of it and allow your experiences in life (your setup) to bring you closer to your purpose (your punchline). I'll be honest, it may not always be easy. I'm a comedian, not an auctioneer. Walking back onto that stage time and time again to raise money that night was one thing that stretched me most at that time in my career. There was tremendous risk. But I'm so glad I did it. It certainly was worth it.

The risk you need to take to deliver your punchline will always be minimized when you don't confuse the vehicle with the destination.

Whenever you feel a prompting to help others in some way, I want to encourage you to step from behind your curtain and go for it. It may not be comfortable, but it will be worthwhile. You've probably heard the phrase, "The greater the risk, the greater the reward", well, I believe this is true times ten when the risk is taken to help another person.

See for yourself! You can watch the whole thing online at *FunnyHowLifeWorks.com/fundraiser*.

CHAPTER 15

BUT CAN YOU BE FUNNY IN PRISON?

I've played to a lot of different crowds in my career: comedy clubs, night clubs, churches, homeless shelters, birthday parties—you name it, I've played it. But one of the toughest sets I ever had was in a prison in Washington State.

Fresh off the revelation that I didn't want to try to *get* laughs, but *give* people an opportunity to laugh, I was feeling great. After having wowed a few homeless shelters, I had even come up with a slogan, or a mantra if you will: "Making laughter commonplace in uncommon places." I was actually feeling pretty good about this and ready to take on whatever comedic challenge was set before me. "Be careful what you ask for," once said by a guy who asked for something and was sorry he asked after getting it. For some reason, everything changed when an actual possibility presented itself. I mean, it seemed like a great idea, sounded awesome when I told my friends what I was going to do, and it was a pretty impressive social media post—but when the day of the set actually arrived, I wasn't so sure I had thought this all the way through. When you see razor wire, electrical fences, and armed guard towers, you start 14th guessing yourself. I would say "second guessing," but my mind was moving much faster than that.

The biggest problem I encountered was doing the math on what jokes could prisoners relate to. I didn't think I could riff about having kids when these men were isolated from their kids. I didn't know if I could jump into comedy about relationships—prisoners were restricted to letters and an occasional visit. And for reasons I won't go into, I certainly did not what to start out with my newly written joke about dating.

As I drove up to the prison, and began the burdensome task of checking in, I was looking at every aspect of the joke-making process only to realize I couldn't use any of my jokes because most of these guys had been here for a very long time, and their entrance to this prison probably looked different from mine. I had nothing: no jokes ready, no idea how this was going to work, clueless as to what I was going to say. It wasn't that I hadn't tried to be prepared ahead of time, it's just that I hadn't had an opportunity to see the venue or get a feel for the audience like I normally would before a show. There was no sound check, no preshow video reel, no watching my opening act. It was pretty unsettling to say the least.

Have you ever found yourself in that type of a situation? You probably haven't done stand-up in lockdown, but I'm talking about a situation where you weren't sure what to say or what to do? Maybe you were walking into a meeting at work and you had no idea what to contribute. Or perhaps you had to confront a friend but didn't know exactly what to say? Well, let me tell you what happened for me . . . and maybe this will give you a little courage next time you're in one of those situations.

As I prepared to enter the prison, the warden took my belt. He said it could be used as a weapon or as a noose. I was nervous already. This was not exactly the reassurance I was looking for. I'm thinking, *Why can't they just boo me like a normal disgruntled audience?* Things only got worse when I heard the first of eight sets of steel doors slam loudly behind me as I walked into the prison.

I was scared . . . for real. I've seen *The Shawshank Redemption*. I knew what kind of things happened in a place like this. I kept listening for Morgan Freeman's voice to calm my nerves, but the *Shawshank* narrator was nowhere to be found.

The further I went into the prison—with each new set of doors slamming behind me—the more uncertain

I became. *What was I going to say?!?* I kept rehearsing jokes in my mind, but I knew none of them would work. These cats were expecting me to bring the funny . . . and I was just focused on holding my beltless pants up. Not exactly the image I wanted to portray.

Deep into the prison, as we neared the room I would be playing, the guards started peeling away. As we went through each set of bars, I would lose a guard or two. When we got to the last set of bars, the two remaining guards told me, "This is as far as we go." Then they gave me a black box with a pin in it, saying, "If the prisoners rush you, pull the pin, and we'll come in and help." Now right here, I need you to remember that part of my gift is to be creative. However, sometimes your gift can seem to work against you. This "gift" of creativity had the following thoughts running through my mind: *A black box with a pin in it. Don't the prisoners know about the pin too? They will grab the pin first. I can't walk in there with my hand on the pin like in a Clint Eastwood movie. I don't even know how to whistle. How is pulling the pin really going to help? Is this a grenade I have on my hip? Is this prison like an airplane plummeting toward the ground? That would explain the black box.*

OKAY—I'm back now.

The prisoners were waiting in a medium-sized space when I arrived. They were wearing pink jump suits, which I thought was pretty strange until I remembered I had read somewhere that pink is a color that soothes and calms people. I had a few jokes come to mind about those jumpsuits, but I could tell from the looks on their faces they weren't happy about wearing pink, so I decided to stay away from that topic. All eyes were on me as I approached the middle of the room.

Here I was, only 10 paces away from the stage (which was no stage at all) and I was in a near panic. The prisoners sat in a circle, surrounding where I would stand, and I still didn't know how I was going to start the set. One joke came to my mind—*Well, you guys sure are a captive audience!*—but I quickly decided against that one. No sense in reminding these guys they were in prison right out of the gate.

Eight steps away . . . six steps away . . . three steps away . . . as I approached the middle of the circle, I heard one prisoner mumble, "This better be funny, *#$&^@#*$&!" I'm thinking: *Did we meet in Flint?*

Showtime.

With microphone in hand, I looked around the room, and my mind started to work in overdrive. In a matter of only a second or two, I read the crowd, deciphered the mood of the men, and my racing heart began to settle.

And that's when I saw him.

There was an older prisoner with a flowing white beard staring directly at me. I knew I would start with him. "What's your name, sir?" I asked boldly.

"My name is Moses."

Boom! That's all I needed.

The first joke popped right into my head.

"Well, Moses, this is what I want you to do. The next time you see the warden of this prison, I want you to look him directly in the eye and say, 'Let my people go!'"

The whole room exploded in laughter.

That was all I needed. That first joke put us all at ease and it turned out to be a great and overall awesome experience.

I've thought back on that moment many times, asking myself the question, *How did I get that joke that fast? How is it possible that it just came to me out of the blue? There was a lot of pressure, and that joke just showed up out of the blue. How did that happen?*

And I've come to realize why that moment could materialize.

You see, I've always had trouble reading. When I was a kid, I struggled to read the stories that all the other kids were reading with ease. Eventually, I might have been diagnosed with dyslexia, but we couldn't afford such a fancy diagnosis. I knew something wasn't right. Instead of letting that keep me from succeeding, I adapted. I learned at an early age how to see patterns and tendencies with sentences. I couldn't phonetically read the words, but my mind found a way to decipher the words in a different way.

I discovered how to interpret the rhythm of the paragraph, how to anticipate and adjust.

> Dealing with this issue as a child definitely felt like a setback in my life, but what I've come to understand is that setback actually gave me skills that have been a benefit.

I'm able to see things uniquely, make the adjustment, and act quickly on my feet. My mind sees things in an unusual way, and that has been a gift to me in comedy. My reading disability, that seemed like a setback in my childhood, actually is the thing that allows me to succeed in adulthood.

I've come to realize that day in the prison was no different from my days in the classroom. When I stood in front of a hostile crowd, my mind found a way to do what my body couldn't: my mind shifted and found another way to succeed. My supposed setback had actually prepared me for this moment and many other moments to come.

I meet a lot of people who have let their setbacks define who they are instead of using them to get to where they want to go. Rather than using their experiences in pursuit of their goals and dreams, they see those experiences as roadblocks, keeping them from even attempting to move forward. I'm not making light of anyone's pain; setbacks can be difficult to recover from. But I do know from my own experiences that setbacks are only as powerful as you allow them to be. If life gives you lemons . . . nevermind, that's been overused. If life gives you gasoline, you could decide to just complain about the smell or use it to blow something up. Or it could be used as energy to get you down the road to fulfillment.

> What are the things in your past—big or small—that have uniquely prepared you for this moment in time?

- If you had bad parents, or absent parents, couldn't that be the motivation for you to be the parent you never had?

- If you failed in a business endeavor, rather than never trying again, couldn't that teach you invaluable lessons for how to succeed the next time?

- If someone betrayed or left you, are the doors still open for someone better to come along?

The next time you're faced with a challenge, a question, or an opportunity, refuse to freeze up in fear. Instead, draw on the lessons life has taught you. The past is only a prison if you allow it to be. I believe your setbacks are really part of your set up so you can deliver what you are called to deliver.

> Life is like a bow and arrow: the tighter the tension in the bow (the farther you've been set back), the farther the arrow will land (the farther you're going to reach). When you let go of what's behind you, you are free to soar forward.

When I was in that prison and had one step left until I had to speak, I didn't know what to say until I lifted my foot up and set it down. It wasn't until my feet were where they needed to be that I could do what I was called to do. When you find yourself in a position where you don't know what to say or what to do, take a deep breath, assess the situation, take that last step, and trust that your own "Moses" joke will come to your mind just in time.

CHAPTER 16

I MADE A SUPERHERO LAUGH

What if I told you I once made a superhero laugh? Would you be impressed? It wasn't Superman; he can see through any joke. It wasn't Ant-Man; my jokes go right over his head. And it definitely wasn't the Hulk; that brotha got anger issues.

I made Spider-Man laugh. And it was the highlight of my professional life. Let me explain.

As I continued to ask how I could *give* people an opportunity to laugh, I found more and more opportunities to serve. Still keynote speaking and playing in clubs, I was also doing my act in prisons, juvenile detention facilities, foster care, and youth jails—all places where people are waiting for their time to be up.

I've enjoyed all of those experiences, but none of them compare to the show I did at The Dolphin House, a children's home in Montrose, Colorado. When a dolphin is injured, other dolphins swim around it to protect it until it's healed. This is what The Dolphin House does for children who have suffered abuse. These kids' stories are not only heartbreaking because of what they've had to endure, but also because most of them have been robbed of the ability to live carefree, which is a key ingredient of being a kid. Drug addicted parents, abandonment, physical abuse, sexual abuse—they've been through some of the worst things you can imagine.

Because I wanted to know how to approach my set, I sat down with the caretakers, employees, and volunteers before my event and listened to the stories. I had a feeling that knowing these details might make it harder to present my act, but I felt it was more important to connect than to perform. I was so taken aback by the tragic things these adorable kids had gone through that I quickly started feeling physically and emotionally drained before I even took the stage.

One story in particular stood out to me. A grandmother, who also volunteered at the facility, told me about her grandson who would be in attendance for my show. She continually toggled between smiles and tears as she told me about the six-year-old joy in her life, her grandson, while intertwining instances of the hurtful truths and pain of the child's mom being strung out on drugs. When the mother was high, she would physically abuse him—specifically, she would pull out his toenails. I was speechless. *How was I going to tell jokes to kids who had been through so much?* The grandmother went on to share with me, "Michael Jr., I just want to warn you. You won't see his face at your show tonight. See, he wears a Spider-Man costume everywhere he goes because he is so afraid. He hides behind that mask and doesn't take it off."

As expected, the room was full of the children, their caregivers, social workers, and volunteers. And sitting right up front, clinging to his grandmother while seated on her lap, was a six-year-old Spider-Man.

I knew before arriving that I couldn't do my regular routines. If I was going to bring laughter to this room, it would have to come from a much deeper place than my head. I was going to have to push past my empathy for them to assess the broader situation and bring content that I thought would help children and stressed-out adults laugh. As I stood on stage with mic in hand, I started looking some of the kids in their eyes, recalling their stories. I started thinking to myself, *I can't do this. It's too hard and too heavy. I can't make these people laugh.* Then once again, I was reminded of what I was really there to do. I'm there to *give* them an opportunity to laugh.

> I have the gift of helping people laugh, but a gift isn't really a gift until you give it away expecting nothing in return.

So that's what I did. After taking a really deep breath, I simply presented my gift. And for the first eight minutes or so, the response was mediocre at best. And even though it wasn't going great, I had a peace while doing it that I still cannot explain. After about the ten-minute mark, the laughter started to increase, and it seemed to start with the adults. And as they laughed, I noticed this was almost like a signal to the kids that this was a safe place, and they began to laugh too. Pretty soon everyone was laughing and seemed to be having a great time. Everyone, that is, except for Spider-Man. I wasn't exactly sure how to reach this little guy, especially since I couldn't see his face through the mask. I couldn't look into his eyes. I had no idea how to read what he might be thinking or feeling. So, I took a more deliberate approach. I offered him a gift.

I brought along with me some of my children's books I authored called *The Parts We Play*. I held a book up and explained some of the story in the book to the crowd, then asked Spidey if he wanted to have it. After some hesitation and a nudge from Grandma, the little kid got down off his grandma's lap, cautiously walked to the stage, grabbed the book, and sprinted right back to the safety of her lap. It was a pretty awesome moment that certainly impacted me and seemed to change the temperament of the entire room. The laughter went to another level. I can't explain exactly why. The only thing that was really different was that I had given something away. Maybe these kids weren't used to someone giving them something and expecting nothing in return. Maybe it was the feeling of laughter in the room, or maybe they thought I was a black Santa Claus. What I do know is that from that moment on things were different; we all felt closer for some reason.

The room was filled with laughter, but little did we know our time together was about to hit a new plateau that none of us could have imagined. After delivering another punchline, the laughs started to quiet down. Then I heard a little voice coming from the direction of the grandmother that was trying to get my attention. As I turned and looked, standing there with his little chest poked out was our six-year-old superhero, only he was no longer wearing his mask. He looked me in my eyes and stated in a strong a clear voice, "My name is Ronin!"

We were all simply stunned. It was all I could do to keep my suddenly blurred vision from quickly turning to tears. To this day, it is one of the most powerful moments in my comedy career.

After he made his statement, it was as if the floodgates opened, and Ronin, formally known as Peter Parker, went on to tell me everything about himself. I wasn't talking to Spider-Man or Peter Parker any longer. I was talking to an adorable six-year-old boy named Ronin. The visual transformation was truly amazing. By the end of the night Ronin and I were on stage breakdancing together.

I'm pretty sure I could end this story here and we would all be satisfied, but at the risk of sounding like an infomercial, "but wait, there's more . . ."

Over a year later, I received a letter from Ronin's grandmother. It was a simple, heartfelt note that said, "Michael, I just want you to know that since that day you shared your comedy with us, Ronin never put his mask on again. Not once."

I think about that day at The Dolphin House a lot.

We all have a gift to give. Whether it's our talent, our ideas, our experience, our time—every single person has something they can share with the world around us.

But I've found that many times we only look for ways to share those gifts with people who can afford it, people who can pay us, or have somehow earned it. We might not consciously make that decision; it seems to happen by default. But something truly life-changing happens when we share our gifts with those people who can never pay us back.

And here's the thing: I'm not just talking about helping those in prisons, detention centers, hospitals, shelters, and children homes (though those are great places to serve). Anybody who can't pay you back is a perfect candidate for you to share your gift; many times, it's the marginalized, the hurting, and the struggling. But there are times it can be those who seem to have it all. When you look beyond the monetary and ask, "What can I give?", you may find that the people who need to receive from you are those closest to you. Your boss, your cousin, your mom, or your best friend.

Ronin wore a mask because he felt it protected him and helped him feel strong. There are many people who wear a mask for these exact reasons, but their mask looks like anger, frustration, cutting you off in traffic, yelling, rejection, arrogance, and fearfulness. There are many masks people wear on the outside to hide the hurt they are feeling on the inside. The best way to let them know that they are in a safe place is to be willing to show up with gifts like love, understanding, patience, kindness, and encouragement. I believe when you work to deliver these gifts, expecting nothing in return, those you give to just may reveal their true identity.

The day I made Spider-Man laugh inspired me to look around every day for ways to deliver to someone else. I hope it has done the same for you.

See for yourself! You can watch the whole thing at *FunnyHowLifeWorks.com/spiderman*.

CHAPTER 17

HE DECIDED TO PROPOSE AT MY COMEDY SHOW

I've had a lot of interesting (and sometimes crazy) things happen during my keynotes and comedy shows, and you're getting a glimpse into some of those things in this book. One of those experiences was a wedding proposal that happened on stage. It wasn't my proposal—for the most part I was a bystander like everyone in the crowd that night—but I was kind of nervous . . . because it was all my idea. Let me explain.

I've always felt a comedy show was a good place to propose, because if she says "No," you can be like, "Ha, ha! I was just joking. Yeah, let's go get some nachos." But I had never seen one until this particular day.

The whole thing was set in motion earlier in the day. I had done a presentation, not really a comedy set, to a group of people that morning. During my talk I got a little personal, telling the crowd about the reading problem I had as a kid. I told those in attendance that my reading challenges as a kid actually turned out to be a blessing because they became practice for me to look at things differently. I learned to read by looking at the words in a different manner than the other kids, and that's basically what comedy is—observing life differently than other people. My reading setback was actually practice for the punchline God had for me later. After sharing my experience, I said these words:

> "Everyone, in some form or another, has had some sort of setback that may have brought them a lot of pain. I don't want to take from the truth that it was hard to deal with; however, . . .

. . . if you can allow yourself to get to a place to change your perspective, you could see that experience was preparation, or practice if you will, for something great.

That very thing that was meant to harm you can be used for good. For some people, maybe your setback was that you never met your dad, or your parents were divorced. Maybe you were mistreated as a child, or maybe your mom was an alcoholic. Whatever the case was, if you can allow yourself to change your perspective, you can use that situation for your benefit, and to the benefit of others as well."

After the presentation, I was signing autographs and noticed a dude hanging around near the autograph line waiting to talk to me. After the line cleared, he walked right up to me, and I could tell he had been crying, and even now he seemed to be holding back tears. He said to me, "Michael Jr., you don't understand how much that talk meant to me. You see, pretty much all of those things are what happened to me, and I never thought to ask, 'How can these things be used to help others and myself?' So, these tears are because I am feeling overwhelmed with thoughts of how my dark past can bring so much light to my future."

I was really blessed by his honesty and newfound clarity and immediately felt connected. We began talking about life and how God could use his setbacks as a setup for his punchline. It was a really great conversation, and after a few minutes of talking, this sweet little five- or six-year-old girl ran up and grabbed his hand and rested her little blonde head against the side of his leg. He embraced her and called her "Sweety."

"Is this your daughter?" I asked.

"No, this is actually my girlfriend's daughter."

I can't really explain why I said what I said next, but for some reason it just felt right.

I pulled him aside as the little girl skipped back to her mother who was talking down the hallway to a friend, and asked if I could be brutally real with him. He was receptive to that, leaning into what I was going to say.

"Listen, man, you have to make a decision. That little girl is looking up to you like you are her dad. If you don't actually plan to step up and fully be there for her and marry her mom, then you need to get out of the way so whoever is going to marry her can step into the picture."

Looking back on it, that was a pretty bold thing to say, especially since I hadn't even got his first name yet, but it just felt right at that moment.

> I'm always listening in the gaps for what's really going on—in my comedy and in my life—and somehow, I felt he needed to hear that.

He paused for a moment, and then he told me that he had been wanting to marry her for a while. In fact, he already had a ring but didn't know when the right moment was.

I didn't hesitate. "What are you doing tonight?" I asked.

"What do you mean?"

"I have a comedy show tonight. You could propose to her there! It will just be me, you, and maybe 3,000 humans you have never met before. If you want to do this, we can. I'll work out all the details. Just tell me if you really love her and if you're serious about being committed to her."

He absolutely loved the idea of professing his love to her publicly, so much so his eyes once again started getting watery and then I felt my eyes start to do the same. Then we both shook it off and simultaneously started talking about football. And the plan was set into motion.

So, here's what happened . . .

I couldn't just call him up on stage that night, because his girlfriend and the audience would probably sniff out what was about to happen before he could actually drop to one knee. Besides that, the whole night couldn't be about a proposal. The place was going to be packed out and the people paid good money to be entertained. So, this needed to be a surprise, not just to his girlfriend, but to my fans as well. So, I came up with a plan.

Toward the end of the show, I would ask three seemingly random couples to come up on stage. I would ask these three couples if they enjoyed the show and if they had learned anything about life through the comedy. Then I would ask the guy to share with his lady what he learned and how he might apply it to their relationship to improve things. Now keep in mind, the first two couples were decoys. They were in on the plan so they played their roles perfectly—the last couple would be the proposal. *What could go wrong?*

But there was one potential problem: Because his girlfriend was bringing her daughter to the show, we had to have someone watch the little girl while Couple #3 was on stage. So, to solve this problem, we had my assistant sit next to the couple during the show. When I called them on stage, she would then ask, "Hey, I can keep an eye on her for you?" The boyfriend and I had prearranged this before the event. *Problem solved,* so I thought.

The show went great that night, even though the whole time I was performing, I was doing the math on how to best accomplish our plan at the end of my set. *Was the boyfriend going to follow the plan as we had talked through and just drop to one knee and say, "Will you marry me?" Or would he be too nervous and go into some long drawn out speech that would completely spoil the punchline? Or was this thing about to completely fall apart?*

After finishing the big joke, I would normally close the show with dropping the mic, but instead of dropping the mic, I segued into "project proposal." I randomly called the three couples to come up on stage, including Jamie and his girlfriend, hopefully soon to be wife. This is when the potential calamity struck—the little girl bounded on stage with Jamie. I'm thinking, *Dude! What are you doing?! We talked about this! Leave the kid with the assistant.*

You have to understand; there were already enough unknown variables in place, but a kid on stage? This could be all bad for our plan. Kids are unpredictable. I know this because I used to be one. I had no idea what was about to happen.

It was too late to bail now, so I just put my head down and executed the game plan we had talked about. I asked Couple #1 if they had enjoyed the show and what they had learned. Then I asked the man to tell his wife what he wanted to do to make their relationship better. He gave a great response and the crowd ate it up. Then I did the same thing with Couple #2. They, too, had enjoyed the show and the husband also said something uplifting to his wife.

Now it was showtime . . .

Couple #3, daughter in tow, now known as Jamie and Allison, stood before me. I looked Jamie in his eyes for a few beats to make sure he was still on the same page with me. I couldn't really tell for sure, so I just gave him the cue, "Do you have anything you want to say to Allison?" As he looked into her eyes with her daughter at her side . . .

Remember, the plan was that he was going to immediately drop to one knee and simply say to her,

"Will you marry me?" But unbeknownst to me, he had another plan in mind. In front of 3,000 people as well as their family and friends that we snuck into the back of the room, he got down on one knee, pulled out a ring, looked up into his girlfriend's eyes and then turned to the precious little girl and said, "Can I marry your mommy and be your daddy forever?" WOW!!!!! Now somehow the 3,000 people in the room sounded more like 20,000. Actually, more like 20,000 women who were just shown a picture of a newborn baby holding a puppy while Elton John sang *Can You Feel the Love Tonight*.

It was one of the most precious moments I've ever seen. The entire crowd went crazy. The daughter nodded in approval and said, "Yes." He then turned back to his girlfriend and said, "Will you marry me?"

The girlfriend did what 98% of women would do in that situation. You know the move where women cover half their face with both hands like they suddenly need a breathing mask? Yep, she did that and then said, "Yes!" through an explosion of tears. The crowd went crazy. Her family went crazy. And I went a little crazy, too. I'm pretty sure there was not a dry eye in the room. Even now, recalling this beautiful moment makes me wonder what next year's NFL season will be like for the Detroit Lions.

I've stayed in touch with this couple since that show. They've been married for over two years now, and they're happier than they've ever been in their lives. It just goes to show you that great things can happen at a comedy show.

See for yourself! You can watch the proposal at *FunnyHowLifeWorks.com/proposal*.

CHAPTER 18

THE TOUGHEST ROOM
I EVER PLAYED

It's not super hard to anticipate the things that will go down at a kid's birthday party. Cake and candles, not fully grown humans running all over the place, parents standing around awkwardly, and an off-key rendition of the "Happy Birthday" song. And you don't really expect to learn a life lesson, at least I didn't, but that's exactly what happened.

It was early in the 2000s and my career was doing pretty well. I was playing bigger rooms and my calendar was staying pretty full. Most importantly, I had a new sense of clarity of direction and felt like God wanted me to get there in a non-traditional way.

> **All I needed to do was keep putting in work and trust in Him.**

I got a call from a lady I had met at an event several months earlier. She asked if I would perform at her son's birthday party. Performing at a kid's birthday party is an immediate red nose. I was going to say red flag, but nose is more appropriate as that's what a clown would wear to such an event. But instead of reacting, I just listened for an opportunity to respond, because that's the polite thing to do before hitting someone with a confident "NO."

She went on to explain that the show wouldn't be for the kids, but actually for the adults at the party. But I was still like, "I'm not feeling this." She went on to say, "It will be a well done event because the party is for my preteen son, Trey, and his dad, Will Smith, will be there. Michael Jordan's family will be there. Eddie Murphy will be there. A lot of producers and other celebrities will be there too."

She was clearly hinting that this could be a great move for my career; and as she was talking, I was kind of picking up what she was putting down, so I semi-reluctantly said yes.

As I drove to the venue, I was pretty excited. Michael Jordan! Will Smith! Eddie Murphy! Hollywood producers! Any one of these people could give me the big break I had dreamed of. Not only that, Eddie Murphy was a comedian I had always admired. I remembered watching and listening to him on a regular basis when I was young. He was the comedian who got me interested in comedy in the first place. This was a huge opportunity.

When I showed up at the party, I started to get a sense that this wasn't going to go well, and I was right. For starters, I had helped Trey's mom put together a short video to play at the party. This was something they did every year. Trey was playing flag football at the time, so I came up with an idea to take highlight clips of him playing football and talk about how he was going to go straight from flag football to the NFL. If we played it right, it would be pretty funny, but we had worked on a very limited budget with just one camera dude who gave us just four hours.

When I got to the party, I learned that this was the first year Will Smith and his production team wasn't doing the video. I had zero idea that my flag football video was a replacement.

The second problem was the venue itself. The party was being held at some kind of bowling alley/arcade. It was loud, kids were running around everywhere . . . and there was no stage. *That was a major problem!* When I took the gig, I had explained that I needed a stage with a spotlight and a good sound system. I probably should have clarified exactly what I meant by the words "stage," "good sound system," and "spotlight." Now let me say here that the awesome lady who asked me to do the party is still a good friend of ours and every person we met at the party was amazingly cool, just really nice people. I should have just been clearer about what was really needed for an optimal comedy set. So, instead of a stage, they put two end tables together for me to stand on, and the spotlight was pretty weak. It seemed to get about halfway to me and then ask, "Hey, can you meet me part of the way?" The only light I had was coming from a lamp hanging from the ceiling not quite centered over my new makeshift stage. Eyeballing this from across the room, it seemed that the dangling lamp was not more than 6 feet high from the tops of the end tables. I wasn't 100% sure at the time because I didn't have health insurance and hadn't seen a doctor for a physical exam in years, but I was pretty sure I was six foot two. *This is going to be bad.*

As I stood there having a conversation in my head about how bad would it be if I just left, the kids stopped bowling and playing video games long enough to join their celebrity parents in watching the video. Surprisingly, the video was a hit and people were laughing right at the points I thought they would. After getting this response to the video, I was feeling very encouraged and even confident. That is until I caught another glance of the stage that looked like something Charlie Brown made after his Christmas tree. Looking over at those end tables located in the darkest area of the room, seemed to make the success of the video quickly fade.

At about this time, this guy passes me, slowly heading toward the table-stage and I noticed he had a microphone in his hand. Then with no warning at all, he started to introduce me. Well, he didn't really introduce me—he just said something like, "I'm sure he's a nice person. He's probably going to be funny." This is my intro?? "He's probably going to be funny?" "Ladies and gentlemen, meet Michael Jr."

As I started walking to the end tables, I literally rubbed shoulders with the man who showed me what stand-up comedy was, Mr. Eddie Murphy. And for a beat, things seemed to slow down. So, as I looked Eddie Murphy in his eyes, as the crowd applauded, the only words I could think to utter to him were, "We are both about to see that this is not the place to do stand-up comedy." He had no idea what I was talking about and for sure didn't know who I was. He probably had no idea there was a comedian on the schedule.

I climbed up on the tables only to discover the table on the left had a wobbly leg and the lamp was hanging just above my head. It must have looked like I was wearing a sombrero sideways. As I was standing there for a half a beat, I quickly realized that there was a significant amount of heat coming from the light bulb and that I needed to continually adjust my head to keep from getting burned. After kind of gaining my composure, I discovered a third detail that could make this performance difficult—the sound system. Specifically, there wasn't one. When I started my set, I realized my voice was coming through the bowling alley's PA system. It sounded like I worked at a drive-thru that used to be a McDonald's but had been converted into a Mexican restaurant. So, there I was, straddling two wobbly tables, dodging a swinging heat source, attempting to tell jokes over a crackling PA system that no one could hear because of all the noise at the bowling alley.

For the first two to five minutes, partygoers were really working to give me their attention, but because they couldn't hear a thing I was saying, they quickly lost interest. The kids went back to their games and the adults went back to their conversations. Instead of playing for 120 influential Hollywood personalities, I did 20 minutes for the eight people that were standing closest to the makeshift stage. These people either were really enjoying my performance, or they couldn't deal with the awkwardness of being that close to me and walking away. I should mention that one of the eight was my wife. What I thought could have been an amazing opportunity had turned into a complete bust . . . or so I thought.

This is where the life lesson came in. As I was standing on those end tables trying not to burn my head on the swinging lamp, I felt like God was saying to me, "You thought somebody in this room was going to take you where only I can take you."

> And that's when it hit me: I didn't have to depend on what a person could do for me—I just had to do my part and trust God would do His.

When I realized that, I settled down and had a blast with the eight people right in front of me. What was easily the worst show I would ever have quickly became one of my best comedy experiences ever because of what I learned in that moment.

What about you? Are you looking to a person, a job, or an opportunity to take you where only God can? Here's what I want you to catch: People, circumstances, and opportunities are not what determine your purpose. They are a part of your set up so you can deliver it. When you come to that realization, you'll find a new peace and start walking with even more clarity. I didn't expect to learn this at a birthday party, standing on two wobbly end tables, while being burned by a lamp . . . but I'm glad I did.

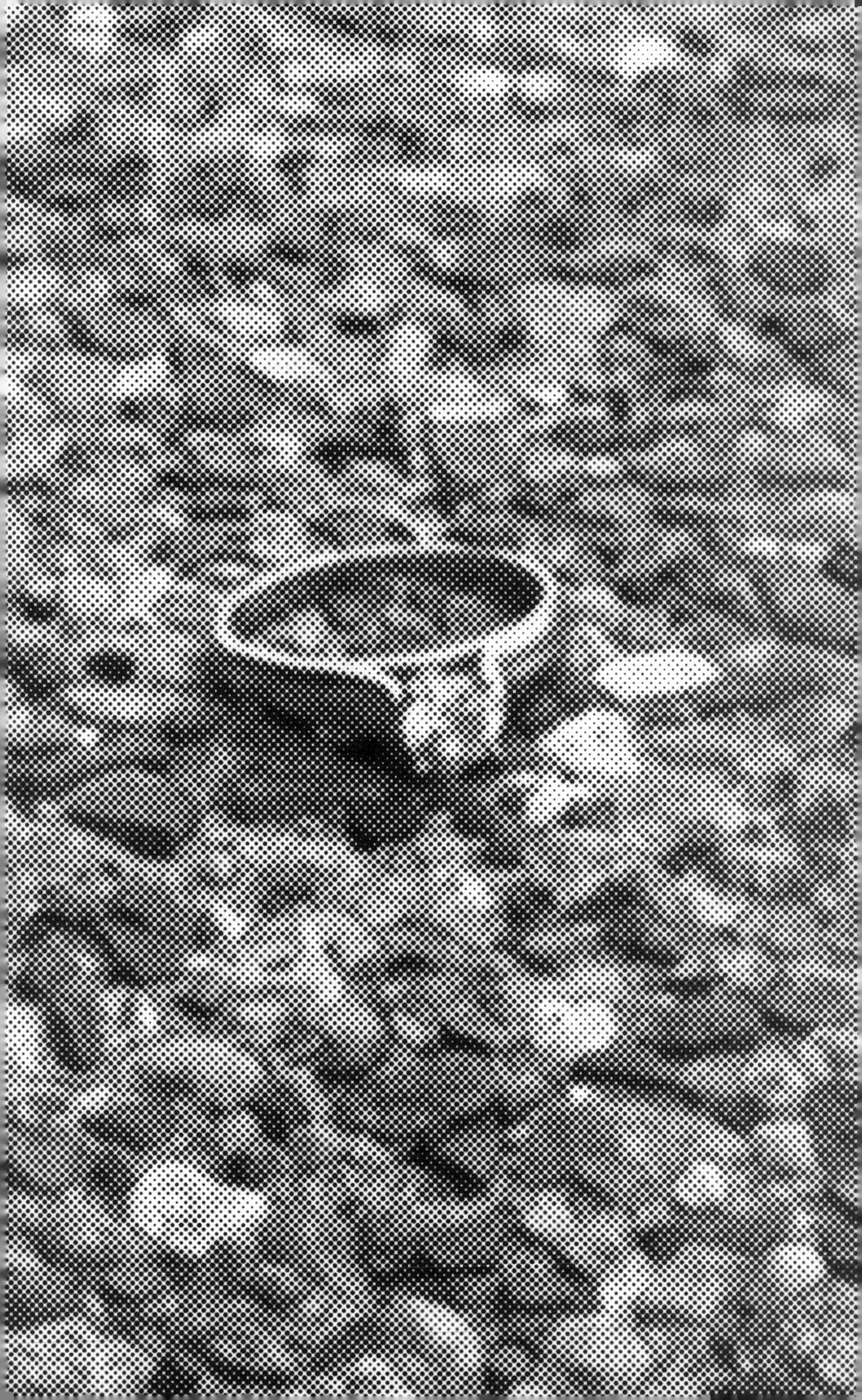

CHAPTER 19

JUST CALL ME
THE LOVE DOCTOR

Comedy is the vehicle, not the destination. Helping people get in a position where they can do more and be more, that's how I like to get down. Comedy affords me a platform to do exactly that: challenge people to find their purpose.

Because I know this is my calling, there are times where I can be pretty bold. Anytime I feel a prompting to challenge someone, that pretty much is what I do. And the results can be incredible: sometimes it's funny, sometimes it's inspirational, and every once in a while, it's absolutely mind-blowing. Kind of like the story I'm about to share next.

Let me start by saying . . . if you are reading this, I am actually surprised as I didn't think this story would make the cut. The reason I say this is because the base of this story is so unbelievable, it actually makes it hard to believe. But it did happen. I was there.

Mind-blowing!

I was scheduled to play a Saturday night show outside of Indianapolis, Indiana. The day started off just like any other travel day. We arrived at the airport the afternoon of the show and a driver picked us up to take us to the hotel. During the drive, we chatted with the driver (we'll call him Tony), and I hit it off with him right away. Tony was a really cool dude. We all laughed together and shared stories en route to the destination. Before getting out of the car, I decided to invite Tony to play basketball with us the next day.

The show went well Saturday night, but it was nothing compared to what was going to happen during the Sunday night show . . . I just didn't know that yet.

Tony picked us up Sunday morning to go play basketball. I like to exercise when I'm on the road and Tony seemed pumped just to be hanging with us. The outdoor court where we were going to play was quite a ways away, so that gave us plenty of time to talk during the ride. Damion, from my team, asked "Hey, Tony man, are you married?"

"Nah, but I have a girlfriend."

"Cool," Damion replied. "How long have you guys been dating?"

"Four years."

When my team heard Tony say he had been dating his girlfriend for four years, they kind of looked at me as I prepared to chime in; they knew the conversation was about to go deeper.

And that's exactly what happened.

Listen, this is NOT something I do all the time, however at this moment, I felt like it was cool to challenge my new friend. Four years is a long time. I couldn't help but speak up.

"Four years?! Man, it's time to make a decision. Your phone has a ring, why doesn't your girlfriend? What are you waiting for?"

Now, I'm not normally this straightforward. I've challenged guys like this once or twice, but it's not like I'm just walking up to random dudes and telling them to get married. But Tony seemed like he was open to the input and looking for some direction; and I felt like the time was right to give him a little nudge.

He started getting emotional, so he pulled the car over to the side of the street. I'm thinking, *Dude, I still want to play ball before the show though*. He looked at me and said, "Man, you're right. I do need to marry her. I mean, I really do love her, but . . . never mind."

Then after looking puzzled and a little sad for a bit, he put the car back in Drive and we headed to the basketball courts. As we were driving along in silence, you didn't have to be a detective to know Tony was in deep thought. That's when he said, "Michael, I'd marry her today if I could, but the problem is I don't have a ring to give her. I want to give her something nice. She deserves something special, and I don't have that kind of money."

To me that wasn't a problem. I challenged him, "Man, you can get a ring anywhere and attach a meaning to it to make it special. You could get her a ring out of a bubble gum machine and say to her, 'You know how sometimes gum will stick to your shoe? Well, that is how my heart is stuck on you.' Well maybe not exactly that, but you understand. If she really loves you, she will see it's not about where you are right now; it's about where you both can get to together.

> When your heart is in the right place, the only thing really left to do is trust God. There's a saying 'the devil is in the details,' well that's why I let God take care of them."

Then I took it a step further . . .

"If you get a ring today, I'll bring you up onstage during tonight's show and let you propose during my set."

He seemed excited about this as a possibility and I was excited because we arrived at the basketball courts.

These courts seemed to be out in the middle of nowhere. We all warmed up, picked teams, and started playing. By game two, I had crossed over four different players causing their ankles to sprain and dunked on two seven-footers; no need to fact check this part because that's not what this story is really about. My friends and I were into the game, but I could tell Tony wasn't really feeling it. He was obviously distracted.

During a break between games, Tony brought up the topic of his proposal again. Sweating and out of breath, he said, "Man, I'm excited to propose, but I just don't know where I'm going to find a ring. It seems impossible."

I wasn't the least bit worried about it. You see, my late friend, Brian Klemmer, used to say, "When the intention is clear, the mechanism will appear." In other words, when your intentions line up with God's intentions, He will take care of the details. I had no idea what was about to happen. I was just thinking Tony could fashion a ring out of a soda can top or something. To me, the cost of the ring didn't matter—it was simply about following love. I shared that with Tony and told him not to sweat it. If he could come up with a ring or not, I was still willing to bring him on stage that night to give his girlfriend the proposal of a lifetime.

We went back onto the court to play another game. I started dribbling, getting ready to pass the ball, when a reflection from the ground caught the corner of my eye. I didn't pay it much mind at first because the ball was passed back to me and I had to dribble behind my back to spot the defense and use my left hand to score on some guy named Zion; but again, not important to the real story. After blocking the James Harden's (Houston Rockets) shot on the other end, I was bringing the ball back up and saw the shiny object again. "Yo, hold up," I said, walking over to investigate what was hidden in a crack of the cement.

As my eyes focused in disbelief, I just looked down at the ground, then down the court at Tony, then kind of up toward the sky. As all the men circled in, it must have looked like a scene from the movie *Goonies,* or is it *The Sandlot*? I picked it up; and yep, it was a diamond ring.

We all looked at it in silence for a few beats. Then with no words, I handed it to Tony. We all went crazy and started jumping up and down and pushing Tony around in celebration as the smile on his face grew from amazement to joy.

This was impossible. How could something that crazy actually happen? We were looking around to see if this was some kind of setup. *Who finds a diamond ring in the middle of nowhere?*

Now none of us on the basketball court were diamond experts that day so I have no idea what the monetary value of the ring was, but here was what I told Tony, "Dude, I don't know if that diamond is legit or not, but it's not the ring that has to be real for your relationship to work; it's your love and commitment that has to be authentic." To me, that ring is invaluable now because of the story it represents. When you line your heart up with God's and choose to do what you feel is right, God takes care of the details. If you are reading this and you are married, let this ring represent that theme.

That night, still blown away by what happened on the basketball court earlier in the day, I called Tony up on stage. It went down like this . . .

I started improvising with some other audience members and creating funny off the cuff, then I made my way over to the person I really wanted to talk to, Tony.

Me: *Hey, man, what's your name? (Like we never met before)*
Tony: *I'm Tony.*
Me: *Cool. Hey, how tall are you?*
Tony: *6'2"*
Me: *No, you are not 6'2". I'm 6'2".*
Tony: *Yes, I am. I got a physical a little while ago.*
Me: *Really? Stand up so I can see.*

Tony stood up.
Me: *You are not 6'2". I can't tell from where you are. Can you come up on stage please? I don't think you are even close to 6'2".*

Tony came up on stage and stood next to me. We were clearly the same height.

Me: *Well, looks like you are 6'2". Well, as long as I got you up here . . . want to play a game?*

Tony: *Sure, I'm down.*

Me: *So, it's a two-player game. Do you have a friend or someone here with you who can play too?*

Tony: *I have a girlfriend.*

Me: *Awesome. Is she here?*

Tony: *Yeah, she's here with me tonight.*

Me: *Bring her up. We need another person to play this game.*

Tony's girlfriend comes on the stage.

Me: *Yo, Tony, hold this microphone for me for one second.*

As soon as I handed Tony the mic, I stepped to the side. He looked at his girlfriend, dropped to one knee, and pulled out the ring. The crowd went berserk.

The fact that Tony was willing to do the right thing even though he didn't have all the details was a huge step.

> Sometimes that's how we have to roll. We just need to take the next step even when we don't have everything figured out. We just have to be willing to believe it's going to work out.

I've never told that story on stage before because it sounds too impossible to be true, but aside from my slightly elevated basketball skills, and the appearance of an NBA player in the game, it is actually 100% what happened that day. It was a moment I'll never forget. For me, it's a reminder that when you make the decision to do the right thing, God will always work out the details—when the intention is clear, the mechanism will appear.

If there is a dream or a purpose in your heart but the circumstances around you make it seem impossible, let Tony's story encourage you today. The right person is still out there, the career break can still happen, the friendship can be restored, the hard work can still pay off—you never know what you might find in the cracks of life.

CHAPTER 20

"I GET IT NOW."

Have you ever had someone come up to you and say something strange? Something completely random? I have. And I have to tell you about it . . .

"Do you remember me?"

A lady came up to me after a show one night and asked that very question: "Do you remember me?" Even though I don't really have a particularly colorful past, when women in your autograph line say this, it can make you pause for a beat. Sounds kind of weird when you think about it. I meet a lot of people as I travel the world doing comedy, so it's hard to remember everyone I've met, but the truth was that I *did* remember this lady. How could I forget?!

Let's rewind about a year and a half before that question. I had played a show in Peoria, Illinois. During that show in Peoria, I remember talking for a few minutes about the very things I'm writing about in this book—how the things that happen in your life can be used as the setup for your punchline. I explained to the crowd that a joke was all about *setup* then *punchline*, and life is that way too.

> If you want to find your purpose in life, it's important to use your talents, skills, situations, and circumstances to pursue your purpose . . . aka, your punchline.

Now, the show in Peoria wasn't *entirely* about finding your life's purpose. It wasn't a church service; it was a comedy show. It's not like we were sitting around singing "Kumbaya." We had a great night of laughs . . . but there were a few minutes where I shared some life application.

Anyway, after the show, I was signing books and talking with people when this lady walked up to me and said very dramatically, "I get it now." Then she just walked away. It seemed so strange at the time. I didn't have any idea what this woman was talking about. I remember thinking, *I get it too. You're a little weird.*

And here she was again, a year and a half later, asking, "Do you remember me?" I said, "Of course I remember you. How could I forget?!" She asked if I had a couple of minutes for her to explain what happened that night. I was so intrigued that, even though there was a line full of people waiting to get my autograph, there was no way I was going to say no.

This lady was a high school teacher. She told me that on the night of my show she was broke. Actually, she was broker than broke—her checking account had a balance of negative $132. She couldn't even afford the comedy show ticket, but a friend bought one for her because he knew she needed a night to laugh and relieve the stress she was dealing with at least for a little while.

That Friday, before she came to my show, one of her students told this teacher she wasn't coming back. The student's mom was going to prison and she had never met her father. With no place to live and afraid she might end up in the system, her student was going to just run off and figure out what to do next. When she left class that day, the student said, "You won't see me again. Goodbye."

The teacher said, "Michael Jr., that night, you said that we all have something to deliver to someone, and that's when I knew what I had to do. That's why I came up to you and said, 'I get it now.' I called my student right after the show and told her she could come live with me for a little while."

"I get it now" was starting to make more sense.

This teenage girl, without her mother or father, took her teacher up on the offer. She moved in with her the very next day. But here is the crazy thing: When the teacher was helping her student unpack, she found a suicide note . . . and it had been dated for that Friday, the same date of my event a year and a half ago.

The I-Get-it-Now lady said, "She's here with me tonight. I want you to meet her." I can't tell you how blown away I was. Here was this young lady who had been given a second chance at life because of a teacher who cared enough to go the extra mile.

I met the high schooler and she told me how her teacher had taken the extraordinary step of adopting both her and her younger brother.

> Life had turned from bleak and hopeless to full of opportunity . . . all because an underpaid teacher with a heart of gold realized she had something to deliver.

I think that's more than a good story; I think that's an example for us to follow. We may not be able to take someone into our homes, but there are other ways you and I can deliver a punchline for someone. I am tempted now to riddle off a bunch of examples of ways that you can deliver what you have to give; but instead, I'm asking you to pause right now and literally take about three minutes and come up with something you can do to help someone you have encountered recently. Like really just take a few beats and do it now.

DO IT NOW, PLEASE.

As I think back on that story, I realize it would have been very easy for that teacher to focus on her own problems. She could have had a pity party because she was broker than broke. No one would have blamed her if she had quit her job and looked for something more profitable. It would have been understandable if she had been so distracted by her own situation that she missed the cry for help her student offered up that day; but I'm so glad she didn't. Her simple act of kindness did more than set an example for you and for me . . . it saved a life.

Just something to think about the next time someone comes up and says something totally random. When you have an encounter with somebody, it automatically makes you a part of their story. Are you going to use your set up to deliver a punchline to make their story more impactful? Take a second to hear what they're really trying to say. Maybe they're crazy; that's always a possibility. Or maybe it's something else. Maybe they just get it now.

CHAPTER 21

SHE STOPPED CRYING

"A cameraman, a father, and a comedian
walk into a delivery room . . ."

Although this may sound like the beginning of a joke, it's not. It's actually the beginning of one of the most powerful moments and life lessons I've ever experienced. When I walked into the delivery room that day, I was actually all three of these people—the cameraman, the father, and the comedian—and what I was about to experience was so powerful that Oprah Winfrey asked me if she could share the video on her show. (Spoiler alert: I said yes.*)

The occasion was the birth of our youngest daughter, Portland. I was excited to meet her face-to-face for the first time. I had spent what seemed like 25 months singing and telling her stories while she grew in the comfort of her mother's womb, and I couldn't wait to see her and hold her. I bet my wife could probably be a Navy Seal if she wanted. She opted for a natural childbirth, and she was completely amazing. I have so much respect for the strength of women . . . I mean, WOW. I had to get a tooth pulled once and requested an epidural. I'm not completely sure how this would help, but it was worth a shot. The delivery was perfect. (My wife is awesome!) Most dads do the same thing in the moments after their child is born: they are either crying in unison with the baby or they turn into Scrappy Doo. Well for me, this was child number five, so I went for option number three, Steven Spielberg, and started video recording.

As I proudly captured the first minutes of my daughter's new life, she began to cry. But this wasn't like a regular cry. I initially thought it was the first Friday of the month at noon and the city was testing the emergency response sirens.

The cry of any baby is hard for a father to hear because we don't really know what to do. I'm thinking: *She can't be cold; they have her under one of those chicken warmer lights they use at fast food restaurants. Does she want to talk about her feelings? Is she hungry? I don't think I'm lactiously prepared for such a request. Does she want some coffee?* The cries of my baby who was just minutes old were even more difficult to bear because I couldn't even pick her up and hold her yet—

the nurse was still cleaning her up and performing the necessary health checks that were required.

So there I was videotaping my daughter crying when all I wanted to do was scoop her up and make her feel safe and loved. Because I couldn't hold her yet, I did the only thing I knew to do—I began to speak to her.

"Portland, it's okay, baby. I'm here. I am right here. It's okay, baby. I am right here."

Immediately, her cry started to soften and seconds later it was gone. It seemed and felt as if the sound of my voice comforted her and calmed her down. I wasn't completely sure if it was the sound of my voice that brought this about, but because she was now quiet, I turned my attention to see how my wife was doing. It was only a few moments later when Portland started grumbling then transitioned into the full-fledged yell, and the coyotes in the distances chimed in. Her cry was at full tilt. Full of concern and a little curiosity, I slowly lifted my voice and start to speak to her again, "Portland, don't cry. It's okay. You're alright. I'm right here. I'm right here. It's okay. I'm right here."

And to my joy-filled shock and surprise, she stopped crying again. *It's my voice?!?!*, I'm thinking to myself as I'm still talking to her. *It's my voice. She is responding to my voice!!!*

In seeing that, I was completely blown away, but not nearly as much as I was about to be. See, as I spoke to her, assuring her of my presence, "I'm right here. I'm here," she laid there in peaceful silence, and I added the phrase I had spoken to her many times while she was in the womb, "I love you, Portland. I love you." And for the first time, she opened her eyes—no crying, no struggle, no fear—just big, beautiful eyes looking for her father.

I've seen a lot of beautiful things in my life, but I've never seen anything as beautiful in response to, "I love you."

You see, it's not just babies who cry. Sometimes, life can be so difficult for all of us that we just want to break down. Uncertainty, relationship struggles, career questions, betrayal, heartbreak, fear, or doubt—these things can cause us to feel overwhelmed, all alone, and we struggle to find our punchline (our purpose).

> **But the solution may be easier than you think. Maybe you just need to be still and listen for your heavenly Father's voice.**

It may seem like you're all alone . . .

It could feel like the tears will never stop . . .

It might look like you don't have a future . . .

But He wants you to know, "I'm right here.
I'm right here." He loves you. All you have to do
is open your eyes."

*See the actual video from the delivery room here:
FunnyHowLifeWorks.com/deliveryroom.

CHAPTER 22

THE DEAF LADY THAT MADE US LISTEN

The best punchlines are the ones that the audience never sees coming. This is true in comedy, and it's true in life. A perfect example of that is what happened on a Saturday night at my show in Nashville, Tennessee. This impacted me so much I know I was really an audience member because there was no way I saw this coming.

As I mentioned before, when I first started out in comedy, I was all about *getting* laughs from people. And after I made a major shift, I started asking a different question, "How can I *give* this audience an opportunity to laugh?" Well, at a sold-out event in Nashville, this question got tweaked even more, if not perfected. I started asking the question, "What can I give to this audience?" I found myself asking this question before getting on stage, but while I was on stage as well. I started doing what I called "listening between the gaps." You see, at least a few times a show while the audience was laughing, instead of doing the math on what joke would get the most laughs next, I would ask the question, "What can I give to this audience?" Most of the time it was another joke, sometimes it was some inspiring encouragement, and once in a while it was something even more. And that night in Nashville was looking like an "even more" night. Something incredible happened during that set that I'll never forget—all because I listened between the gaps.

It was a sold-out show, around 2,200 people in attendance. I remember that the set was going very well. Lots of laughs. Everyone was having a great time. I had just delivered a punchline and the roar of laughter had not yet peaked, so I thought to myself, *What can I give to this audience?* And that's when I noticed her. There was a white lady in her mid-50s sitting close to the front about twenty feet to my right. For some reason she caught my attention; and I still can't explain it, but I immediately felt like I was supposed to ask her to come on stage.

Now you have to understand, I rarely bring anyone on stage with me without having a clear understanding as to why and what the plan is. As the laughter started to slow, I told another joke and attempted to observe her as I panned the crowd. Upon this second glance, I noticed that she was hearing impaired and all her attention had really been on the sign language interpreter. I'm thinking to myself, *How is this going to work?* The only sign language I knew was the thumbs up, and another hand jester that I choose to no longer use or even describe here.

So, without knowing exactly why or what was going to happen next, through the interpreter, I asked the woman to join me on stage; and as expected, the whole room got quiet. No one (including me) knew what was about to happen. *Would this be funny? Would this be sad? What was this dude thinking?!?!*

I have to admit, I got a little nervous. I wasn't sure how this was going to play out.

> That's the great thing about listening between the gaps–it's all about opportunity.

If I'm just running through a list of jokes, I know what kind of reaction I'm going to receive; but when I stop to listen to what a person or a crowd needs, there is an opportunity for even bigger laughs, or for something unforgettable to happen—the best kind of punchline. And that's exactly what this Nashville audience and I were about to encounter.

So, the three of us are standing on stage, and the audience that was moments earlier roaring in their seats was now completely silent. Having no idea what to do next, I just took a deep breath and asked through her interpreter, "Can you please tell me, what is your biggest need?" That's not exactly laughter material, but it's the question I felt I should ask.

She signed in response. "I don't have any needs. I'm okay really."

I could see audience members shifting in their seats uncomfortably. But rather than crack a joke, I instructed the interpreter, "Ask her again." So she did.

The woman thought for a moment and then signed that she and her husband had not had a vacation in over 13 years, not even for a weekend. When the interpreter told us about this need, I knew what I had to do.

Now, the easy (and probably obvious) thing to do would be to pass a hat around the room and raise the money on the spot so this woman and her husband could go on a vacation, but the best punchlines are the ones you never see coming. Plus, giving money is not really a punchline; it's just the result of someone leveraging their setup for monetary gain.

So, instead of having a "Go Fund Me" moment right there in the middle of the show, I felt there was a different way to proceed. I simply asked the next question. "Why not?" What had kept this couple from ever taking a vacation?

The interpreter watched the answer carefully and then, with tears swelling in her eyes, told me the couple had a special needs child and they couldn't afford a qualified caregiver to watch their child while they got away for a few days.

So, after being quiet for a few beats, I took another deep breath, walked to the very edge of the stage, panned the room for a few seconds, and asked the audience, "Where is the special needs nurse who can deliver their punchline?"

Silence.

I'm guessing the audience was kind of in shock at the transition; I mean we were laughing hysterically like four minutes ago, so I asked again.

"Where is the special needs nurse who can deliver their punchline?"

The room was one hundred percent silent for about four seconds, then we heard it. We all heard what sounded like a melody as a soft voice made its way to us from the top balcony. "Here I am. I'm right here," a woman said as she made her way to the stage. The audience, including myself, was in awe. I introduced the caregiver to the hearing-impaired woman. As it turned out, they only lived 30 minutes apart. The place exploded in applause, tears, and laughter. Right there, in the middle of the comedy show, they made plans for the nurse to take a few days to watch the couple's child so the hearing impaired woman and her husband could take a much-needed getaway.

I was trippin'. The audience was stunned. It felt like we were experiencing a miracle. And the best part was . . . we didn't just hear about it, we were all part of it.

It's funny how life works, isn't it? A comedy show turned into a moment none of us will soon forget. The biggest punchline of the night didn't *get* laughs, it *gave* us inspiration. And the punchline didn't come from me, it came from a nurse who understood her setup and was willing to deliver her punchline.

> By the way, whatever you do in life, whether at home, work, school, or wherever there are gaps—my question to you is, "Are you listening between the gaps? Are you asking what you can give, or what you can get?"

I want you to think of someone that you love but you really don't express this to them. Go ahead. I want you to actually think about a person who fits this description in your life: could be your mom, sister, a neighbor, or your spouse. Don't continue reading this book until you have this person in mind. What's the person's name? Okay.

Now, without sending it yet, I want you to put in the body of an email or text message the following words: "I just want to say I love you and appreciate you, and I am sorry I don't say this enough." Now I want you to think about the first thought that came to your mind when you thought about sending this? Was it, *Well, this is going to be awkward*; or, *They will think something is wrong with me;* or, *This could really make them happy*. What I'm asking is, did you first think about you or them? If the thought was about you, it is less likely that you would send this text; but if you think about the person receiving it and how it could make them feel better, the chances of you sending it just skyrocketed. This is how you ask the question *What can I give?* as you listen between the gaps. So . . . are you going to send the text?

If you are still reading this book and didn't consider doing the exercise, your default question is most likely, "What can I get?"

No matter what you do in life, there are always gaps. I just think it's important that you be aware of what question you are asking in between them.

CHAPTER 23

GEORGE CARLIN, MICHAEL RICHARDS, AND FORGIVENESS

Sometimes, comedians deal with a lot while on stage—unruly patrons, overcrowded rooms, bad sound systems, hecklers, hecklers, hecklers. Any one of these things can cause a comedian to lose it. (Did I mention hecklers?) That is what happened to Michael Richards on stage at the Laugh Factory in 2006—he lost it. Infamously, Richards went on a racist tirade directed at some black people in the audience, and I don't know if his career has fully recovered. But I met Michael about a year earlier and discovered that he is a completely different person than the man portrayed on news channels around the world. I want to tell you that story. It's a story about friendship, sharing your faith, and forgiveness. Oh, and it's a story about meeting comedy legend George Carlin too. Let me tell you about it . . .

The first time I met Michael Richards it was a passing introduction and hello. I had played a show in Los Angeles that was a tribute to a famous actor. I did my set, people laughed; it was a good time. After the show, Michael came up and introduced himself. Of course, I knew him as the actor who played Cosmo Kramer on *Seinfeld*, and I was happy to meet him. He told me, "Hey, Michael Jr., you're a funny guy," and that was the end of it.

Fast forward to six months later. I'm scheduled to play one of the best comedy clubs in the country, The Comedy & Magic Club in Hermosa Beach, California, and I'm pretty excited about it. This is absolutely my favorite comedy club. The day before my show, I hear that George Carlin is going to do a set the same night. I thought that was really cool because Carlin was a comedy legend and I had never met him. So, yeah, I was pretty hyped.

I was hanging out with some comedian friends who knew where I am with my faith (BTW, in case you didn't know, I love Jesus, and I also love people who don't.), and they told me how Carlin was an atheist. "What are you going to do?" they asked. "Are you going to perform with an atheist?"

I thought they were trippin'. I'm sure I've performed with a lot of atheists before. I'm there to do a comedy show, not argue matters of faith. It's not like we were going to sit around and talk about whether or not God existed.

Little did I know that was exactly the conversation I was going to have . . . just not with George Carlin.

I wasn't too worried about it, but my friends' questions did get me thinking a little bit. Believe me when I tell you, I had no desire of starting a prayer circle in the greenroom, but I did want to be prepared if George brought up the topic of Christianity. I remembered that a speaker at church had given me a little book called *Sharing Jesus Without Fear*. In this booklet, it gave you seven questions to ask people when you share your faith. I flipped through the booklet, trying to commit all seven questions to memory so maybe I would be prepared if the time came to talk about God. Now I am by no means one to try and press my beliefs on others, mainly because I had Christians try to do this to me in the past and it was very strange and awkward. However, if you have read the earlier chapters by now, you know when I feel prompted to do something, I pretty much turn into a pair of Nikes and just do it.

The next night, I showed up for my set at the Comedy & Magic Club and the place was packed out. One comedian opened the show, then the emcee came out and rattled off a few jokes before introducing George. I came out from the greenroom to watch the crowd's reaction as the comedy legend took the stage. The crowd went crazy as they just knew they were in for a special treat.

As the crowd watched, Mr. Carlin went into his last subject matter which was, "Why you should not say, 'God Bless.'" He literally did 15 minutes on the subject. I guess that's to be expected if you don't believe in God. He exited the stage to what felt like mixed reviews, and I was up immediately after him. My first words to the crowd were, "Give it up for the comedy legend George Carlin. God bless him." The crowd exploded in laughter.

After the show, I was back in the greenroom having a great conversation about comedy with George, and Michael Richards walked in. Now this is about six months after my casual introduction to Michael, and I was surprised to see him. Turns out, he had been in the crowd and came back to chat. With me standing right there, he told George, "Someone told me you were playing tonight so I came by to see you, but the craziest thing happened. While I was on my way over here, I had this thought, *I wonder what that guy Michael Jr. is up to.* Then I come down here and there you are on stage. Bam!" When he said, "Bam!" it was like I was talking to Kramer.

(If you believe that God brings people across your path for a reason as I do, you may see where this is going.)

George Carlin, Michael Richards, Mike Lacey (the owner of the club), and I sat around in the greenroom that night and had a great conversation. Initially, nothing about faith came up, and I didn't feel any sense to start that conversation.

After a while, George left, but the rest of us stayed until about 2 a.m. We were having a great time, laughing and talking about all kinds of things. As the night progressed, we started having some pretty deep discussion. Michael actually brought up the subject of faith, so I tried to remember the five questions from the booklet, or wait, were there seven? It didn't matter, because I could only remember two at the time. It's awesome how God makes up for our shortcomings.

"Hey, Michael," I asked. "If you died tomorrow, where would you go?"

Richards didn't even hesitate—he looked at me and snapped his fingers. "You see that," he said. "Once I snap, I can never get it back. It's gone, gone forever." I think he believed our lives were the same way—once you are gone, you're gone forever.

Hmmm. That was question one of my two questions and it didn't seem very effective, so I thought I'd throw the next question at him for the sake of conversation.

"Okay, let me ask you this: If everything you knew about God wasn't true, would you want to know it?"

This question made him think. He sat silently for five or eight seconds, not really having an answer.

That was pretty much the end of our conversation about faith, then the subject changed, and we had some more laughs about life in general.

> When you talk about your beliefs,
> you don't have to push people.
> I believe you can simply plant seeds
> and let God do the rest.

But I think that night I let Michael know that I was always there to talk, and I cared about him as a new friend. The night broke up around 2 a.m. We exchanged numbers and went our separate ways. I wouldn't hear from Michael Richards again for another six months . . . when his face, and the video footage of his on-stage breakdown was plastered on every news channel.

His breakdown was on all the news channels because of his fame combined with his terrible actions that night. He got heckled on stage, and he went completely berserk, saying the n-word and many other racially charged things. It was about as ugly as it could get.

Have you ever felt like you were supposed to do something but you didn't really want to do it? Well, that's how I felt sitting on my couch watching the news of Michael's tirade—I felt like I was supposed to call him . . . but I didn't really want to.

I remember thinking, *What? Why would I call him? I'm not the black person representative. That's like Jesse Jackson or Al Sharpton's job. It's not my responsibility. I do jokes.* But I couldn't shake the sense that I was supposed to call Michael. I didn't even know what I was going to say. I just knew I had to call him.

As I dialed the numbers, I have to be real with you, I was hoping he wasn't going to answer; and thankfully, he didn't. So I left a voicemail:

"Hey, Michael. This is Michael Jr. calling. Hopefully you remember me. Hey, listen, I see what's going on, and I just want you to know that I forgive you. I believe that you are really a good person. If you need anything, give me a call."

Duty done. Phone call made. Now I could go on with my day; but less than ten minutes later, my phone rang. It was Michael's girlfriend. She explained to me that Michael was in really bad shape. He got my voicemail, and he was about to do this press conference, but he wanted to talk to me first.

While waiting on Michael to get on the phone, I turned on the TV. The press was congregated, light bulbs flashing, the podium already set up. The whole world was waiting for Michael Richards to walk out and address the issue, and in the meantime, he was on the phone with me.

I could tell he was hurting and trying not to break down in tears. All he said was, "Buddy, you calling me right now, you'll never know how much that means to me. I have so much hate coming at me right now. You'll never know what your call means."

There was a pause, his voice got even more crackly, and he said, "Thanks buddy. Good-bye." I still had my phone in my hand as he walked out to the podium to offer the world his apology.

I know like I know I have a stronger friend in Michael because of the tough thing that we kind of went through together. Because I forgave him for what he said about me and people who look like me, and then being willing to call, put us on a whole other place that even our joint vocations as comedians couldn't take us. We were able to reconcile in such a great way that now we periodically call each other throughout the year to talk about more than comedy; we talk about life.

If there's anyone that you have a disagreement with, if you can get over the disagreement, in a way, it will actually make your relationship stronger. You'll be stronger than you would have been if you had no conflict at all.

> When a disagreement is followed by understanding, it is confirmation of love.

CHAPTER 24

FROM MY COMEDY SHOW TO PRISON

The things we say and do in life—at home, work, or just hanging with friends—are undoubtedly noticed by others. It seems as if someone is always listening or learning from us . . . especially when we are not aware of it. That's why, as much as possible, every word we say and everything we do should be spoken and carried out with purpose.

Bottom line: You have an effect on others!

I've come to realize this truth from when I'm off stage and for sure when I'm on stage. I sometimes like to stick around after events, talking with people, signing autographs, and hearing their thoughts. Usually, people want to stop by and just let me know they had a good time, but sometimes a person will share something a little deeper. They might tell me about a difficulty they had been going through or tell me this was the first time they had laughed in a very long time. I enjoy hearing these stories, and I consider myself blessed for having a small part in giving them an opportunity to laugh in spite of what they might be going through.

Of all the people who have approached me after a show, there was one man in Roseville, California, who stood out in a big way. He told me something that I'm probably not going to forget for some time!

I was performing for a large audience just outside of Sacramento, California. The show went really well. Standing ovation, people high-fiving each other, the comedy was hitting home and the laughter seemed contagious.

As I went through my set, I took some moments to listen between the gaps, then went off script and shared a few deeper thoughts that I felt might help the audience in a way that the jokes alone couldn't. Again, I've come to learn over the years that sometimes comedy is only a vehicle, not a destination.

> I don't really go on stage with a perfect plan of what it will look like, but I do always go on stage open and willing to deliver whatever I can.

I would say that night about 92% of my material was jokes, and about 6% of what I said went deeper. (That's good math, right?) What I didn't know at the time was this was having a deep impact on one man in particular.

After spending time signing autographs and talking to a lot of folks, I went back to the greenroom to wait on my team who were closing down the merchandise tables. I was relaxing in the greenroom for a few minutes when security told me there was a guy hanging around, asking to speak to me. Like I said, I enjoy talking with people after the show so I went out to talk with this guy. I'm not sure what I was expecting, maybe an autograph or picture request, but I certainly wasn't anticipating what would come next.

I exited the greenroom to find a white guy, wearing an old, dirty t-shirt, kind of standing around nervously. He was covered in tattoos, and his eyes were pretty red, so I was convinced he was high. But as he began to talk, it was obvious he wasn't high after all—he most likely had been emotional.

After I realized he really just seemed to need some help, we stepped to the side a bit to be out of earshot of the security guards and other people, and here's what he told me: "Man, I came to this comedy show to get away from all the stress and pressure. I've got to make some changes in my life."

Now, let me stop right here to say that isn't terribly uncommon. Laughter has a way of opening up people's hearts; so especially when I do an event like this and things are going well, I want it to also be purposeful. If I feel like the timing is right to make a deposit while the heart is open, I just jump. That's what had happened that night.

So, up to this point, everything is cool. But he didn't stop there. He continues: "You see, I left my home state to come to California because I'm a fugitive from the law."

Now that's not a sentence you hear every day. I was blown back! I started looking around for Tommy Lee Jones, "*I want a hard-target search of every gas station, warehouse, farmhouse, henhouse, outhouse, and doghouse.*"

I have to tell you, I've talked to business leaders, soccer moms, blue collar workers, artists, students, other comedians after my shows . . . but "fugitive" was a new addition to my postshow portfolio.

If that wasn't enough, this Eminem-looking brother went on to say, "I'm actually a fugitive of the law in different states. I've been hiding out for the last four months, and after hearing your set, I know I have to turn myself in. Will you help me?"

I'm thinking, *Wow. One of two things must have happened: Either he was so moved by the show, he was persuaded to turn his life around; or he disliked my comedy set so much he'd rather be in prison.*

Either way, I promised I would help him. We spoke for a while, connected and bonded. He said, "This is something I have to do." Some of the security guards were also police officers, so I explained to them what was going on. They placed cuffs on him, and we walked him to the police car. When he got into the back of the cruiser, it was like the end of a movie where the bad guy is driven away, looking out of the window. I was like, *Wow. It really is funny how life works.*

I tell you that story because it is a great reminder that we never know who is listening to what we say or watching how we live. This isn't just true for a comedian who stands on a stage—this is true in your life, too.

> Your words and your actions carry power. You are an example to every single person in your sphere of influence.

When I make an appearance on stage, there is a line of people afterward waiting to talk about what I said and tell me how it affected them. But let's make this personal to you. What would happen if at the end of your day today there were a line of people waiting to talk to you about what you said and did today?

Would they be inspired by what you said and how you showed up, or would they be disappointed, hurt, or confused? Would they be thankful for your encouragement, or would they ask why you ignored them? Would they be better off, even in the smallest way, as a result of your interaction?

This may not be possible with every person you meet, but if you are intentional about doing this, it could be the next time you meet someone.

> The interaction you have with someone can change the next choice they make. That next choice could change their life. Their life could change a community, and that community could change the world.

This could go amazingly well, or as we've seen in the news many times, it could also go pretty wrong.

You may not think what you do or say is important, but it is. Someone is always listening, and you have more influence than you think. This is just one of the things I learned from a fugitive of the law.

CONCLUSION

Man, thank you for reading through this book. I hope I wrote it in such a way that you laughed, felt challenged, and were inspired. Even though we may have never met, I truly do appreciate you. I want you to know that no matter where you are or what you have been through in life, you still have an amazing punchline that you are called to deliver.

If you want to go further in delivering your punchline or gain more clarity on how to, you can get the Funny How Life Works Course at *FunnyHowLifeWorks.com*. In this course, we use laughter to help people understand their purpose. If we can be of service, that would be amazing.

Hold up your phone camera to this QR code to see the message and thank you that I have recorded for you, or you can find it here: *FunnyHowLifeWorks.com/thankyou*.

ACKNOWLEDGMENTS

My amazing wife Ebony – You are _____.
I have no words to express what you mean to me, but I promise to do my best to not only use them all but to express them through actions as we live our lives together. I praise God for you.

Arquist – "Son-that-I-love" as I often call you. Please know that when I sometimes introduce you as "my son with whom I am well pleased," know that this is true, no matter what.

My Tiye – I love you and am blessed by the woman you are growing into. Thank you for being amazing. I love that no matter how old you are, you will jump on my back for a piggyback ride—it's my favorite.

Noka – My oldest and the one who has for sure taught me the most about being a dad, a man, and how to receive love. You are completely awesome, and I smile every time I get to say, "This is my daughter."

Stasha – When you were born, I'm pretty sure my heart skipped a few beats. I love love love you. I get to do comedy throughout the world, but the sound of your laugh is my all-time favorite bar none. Thank you for making it be so easy to be proud of you.

Trin – I love you more than I can begin to explain. You are so brilliant and thoughtful and witty and bold. Even more than this, I appreciate our friendship. I just love being around you pretty much all the time. Thank you, Portland, for being outstanding in so many ways.

TO ALL MY KIDS – As I have said many times in person, I'd also like to tell you here in print: There is nothing you could ever do that would tarnish or diminish my love for you.

This includes all my extra kids as well:
Damion
Shelby
Destiny
Elijah
Damien
Alana

For those reading this that may not know what I mean by "extra kids," I don't have a bunch of baby mamas all over.

These are children, now adults, that God has blessed me to be like a father to over the years.

To my team at Michael Jr. Productions – There is no way I could do any part of this without your help. I know you are "on staff" and being paid, but what you guys do for me in making me better is invaluable, and I love you for it.

To my amazing, amazing parents, Leora and Michael, Sr. – I love you, I love you, I love you. I thank God on a regular basis that He decided to bless me with parents like you.

THE EXTRA CHAPTER

So you must be one of those people who stay in the movie theater enduring the sluggish credit roll in hopes of a bonus scene, while everyone else hits the exits. Cool, I'm one of those people, too. Let's do this.

This story is for sure one of my favorites because I didn't write it. It just kind of showed up as I was crafting some comedy. It is a story about having a relationship with God through His Son. Now if you don't consider yourself a Christian or a religious person, that's cool. I do still think you might get something from it, or at least be remotely entertained.

I'd like to say that this story originally came about when I was journaling in a log cabin on a Colorado mountain top in early spring and this linguistic revelation entered my perception. But that is not at all what happened. I was writing a joke. Yep. I wrote the premise of this joke in my notepad and titled it "The Good Room." Whenever I ask my live audiences, "How many of you know what the good room is?" at most, only one out of five thousand hands may go up. But the truth is, most of them, just like most of you reading this book, know what the good room is. It's that one room in your grandmother's house or your aunt's house, or maybe your house—that one room that's better than the rest of the house. It's where the best furniture and decorations are nicely set up, but nobody can go in. There is usually plastic on the couch and china in a locked cabinet. For the most part, the room is really just for looks, or maybe a super special occasion. Does this ring a bell? Now are you familiar with the good room?

So, I was in the midst of writing this joke, and I felt like God stopped me and told me to tell this story on stage for more than just comedy. (Just like how this book was complete and ready for print, but I feel like I am supposed to add this story for you as well.)

I want you to imagine that you are a house. I know it sounds weird, but if you have found any humor in this book, please return the favor and humor me. Now, where were we? Yes, imagine that you're a house and on the outside of the house is Jesus Christ. He wants to come in, but He'll never force His way in. And He won't just walk in. He wants to be invited in. However, for one reason or another, you will not or have not extended the invitation. In fact, you may think your current setup is just fine. Whenever you need something, or life gets turbulent or uncomfortable, you walk over to the door and just crack it to tell God what's going on and what you need. But that's not a relationship at all. How can you really hear His voice in those circumstances? It's the voice that helps you get out of the pit you might find yourself in. The voice that nudges you when someone near is hurting but they don't know how to ask for what they need. From my own personal experience, I can tell you this all becomes much easier when you do like my fugitive friend in California and just stop running.

> Just surrender to The Authority by simply opening the door and inviting God in.

You may have many reasons why you don't want to let Him in. Or it could be the most common reason I hear from people as I travel the country—because your house is a mess and you think you need to clean it first, or at least tidy it up just a little more. Well, here's a little side note: He can see through the door and through the roof, and He knows what condition your house is really in. He wants to come in and help you put some things in order, but He cannot and will not force His way in. People may try to push their way in while using God's name but know that God will never force His way. He wants you to invite Him in.

There may be things like drugs, adultery, depression, and such in the house. Or maybe you are just buying a bunch of stuff and watching tons of tv, just trying to be distracted. Maybe you brought other relationships into your house thinking that they could at least distract you from the mess, or maybe even help you clean it up. But they can't. The only one who can clean it up is standing outside, wearing an apron with a bucket in His hand, waiting on you to fully open the door.

Then there are some of you reading this right now who used to have Jesus in the whole house. However, over time, whether you realized it or not, you have moved Him to just one room in the house, "The Good Room." Have you ever noticed how the good room, most of the time, is the one with the big window up front so when people look in, they think the whole house is clean?

When people hear about you going to church sometimes, they think the whole house is clean, but you know it is just that one room. You pray and have your favorite Bible verse handy, but it's just that one room. You are a nice person and you even give money to good causes, but it's just that one room. Jesus wants access to the whole house. And if you will open the door and let Him in, He'll not only bring the house back to a brand new state, but you'll have access to hear His voice and continue to make the best choices for your life and those you love. All of this starts with your decision to fully open the door to your heart and invite Him in.

If you want to open your door to God, all you need to do is say this prayer and believe it in your heart:

> Dear God, thank You for sending Your son Jesus Christ to the earth to die for my sins. I also thank You that He rose from the dead on the third day.
>
> Come into my house, come into my heart, and truly have your way in my life now. Amen.

If you prayed that prayer just now, congratulations!! And if you want to know more about what next steps are available, you can text DECISION to 71010.

IF YOU WANT MORE

Michael Jr. comedically inspires people to walk in or toward their purpose. Learn more about how you can live a life fulfilled through online courses, live events, and additional resources. Hold up your phone camera to this QR code, or you can go to: *FunnyHowLifeWorks.com/updates*.